PATRIK IAN MEYER

THE 4 PILLARS OF PROBLEM SOLVING

169 TECHNIQUES & HACKS
TO SOLVE CHALLENGES WITH STRATEGIC THINKING

Build Relationships and Collaborate With People by Fixing Tough Problems Using Creative Solutions

© Copyright 2023 - All rights reserved.

The content contained within this book may not be reproduced, duplicated, or transmitted without direct written permission from the author or the publisher.

Under no circumstances will any blame or legal responsibility be held against the publisher, or author, for any damages, reparation, or monetary loss due to the information contained within this book, either directly or indirectly.

Legal Notice:

This book is copyright protected. It is only for personal use. You cannot amend, distribute, sell, use, quote, or paraphrase any part of this book's content without the author's or publisher's consent.

Disclaimer Notice:

Please note that the information contained within this document is for educational and entertainment purposes only. All effort has been executed to present accurate, up-to-date, reliable, and complete information. No warranties of any kind are declared or implied. Readers acknowledge that the author does not render legal, financial, medical, or professional advice. The content within this book has been derived from various sources. Please consult a licensed professional before attempting any techniques outlined in this book.

By reading this document, the reader agrees that under no circumstances is the author responsible for any direct or indirect losses incurred as a result of the use of the information contained within this document, including, but not limited to, errors, omissions, or inaccuracies.

Table of Contents

Introduction 7

Chapter 1: Problem-Solving Fundamentals 11
    What Is Problem-Solving? 11
    Problem-Solving in Various Fields 14

Pillar 1: Understanding the Problem 19

Chapter 2: Define the Problem 23
    Identify the Problem and Its Symptoms 23
    Clarify the Problem and Its Scope 27
    Define the Problem Statement and Objectives 30

Chapter 3: Analyze the Problem 33
    Identify Causal Factors 33
    Identify Contributing Factors 35
    Conduct a Root Cause Analysis 37

Chapter 4: Gathering Information 43
    Conduct Research 43
    Gather Data 48

Pillar 2: Strategize 51

Chapter 5: Flow Charts & Diagrams 55

    Definition and Importance 55

    Types of Flowcharts and Diagrams 56

Chapter 6: SWOT Analysis 81

    What Is a SWOT Analysis 81

    The SWOT Analysis Process 83

    Limitations & Considerations 85

Chapter 7: Six Sigma Methodology 87

    What Is a Six Sigma Methodology 87

    The Six Sigma Process (DMAIC) 88

    Limitations & Considerations 90

    Variations 91

Pillar 3: Decide 93

Chapter 8: Identifying Options 97

    Conduct Brainstorming Sessions 97

    Probability Analysis 99

    Conduct Idea Generation Workshops 101

Chapter 9: Evaluate and Prioritize Solutions 105

    Decision Matrices and Decision Trees 105

    Develop Evaluation Criteria 106

    Develop Weighting Schemes 107

    Evaluate Alternatives Based on Criteria 109

Chapter 10: Making Decisions 113

    Assessing Risk and Uncertainty 113

Refine and Select the Best Solution 118
Chapter 11: Implementing the Solution 121
    Creating an Action Plan 121
    Developing a Timeline and Milestones 123
    Monitoring Progress 124
    Making Adjustments 126

Pillar 4: Overcome 129
Chapter 12: Lack of Clarity 133
    Identifying Sources of Confusion 133
    Breaking Down the Problem 135
    Refining the Problem Statement and Objectives 137
Chapter 13: Biases & Assumptions 139
    Identifying Potential Sources of Bias and Assumptions ... 139
    Clarifying Assumptions and Defining Key Terms 141
    Questioning Assumptions and Challenging Biases 143
    Gathering Diverse Input 144
    Testing Assumptions and Biases 146
Chapter 14: Time & Resource Constraints 147
    Prioritizing Tasks and Goals 147
    Streamlining Processes and Eliminating Inefficiencies 149
    Utilizing Available Resources Effectively and Efficiently 151
    Creative Problem-Solving and Innovation 152
Conclusion 155
Glossary 157
References 165

Introduction

At the heart of every great achievement lies the ability to solve problems. Everyone faces difficulties in life, both big and small. However, the ability to solve these problems effectively is not something that everybody can do. There are those who struggle with even the simplest of issues. Meanwhile, others have a natural talent for finding solutions. Still, even if you fall into the first category, becoming a more effective problem solver is possible.

Learning to approach problems systematically helps produce optimal solutions and enables you to evaluate these solutions against both short-term and long-term objectives. Recognizing the potential of the right knowledge and strategies empowers you to address even the most complex issues. This ongoing pursuit of knowledge and personal growth motivates you to explore various tools and methodologies that can be pivotal in overcoming challenges. Through such explorations, you are on the path to becoming an adept problem-solver, which is the core theme of this book.

In this book, you will find 169 techniques, tips, and strategies on approaching problem-solving from a new perspective. They're peppered throughout the entire book and it's intentionally designed this way to serve as your guide along each step of the process. The four pillars this book contains will shift how you perceive problems and give you a practical framework for any situation. For instance, it will provide ways to define and break the problem into manageable parts. But this book is not just filled with theories and science; it also offers practical strategies to apply beyond the classroom. Thus, applicable even to address everyday problems in your personal and professional life.

Bumping into life's obstacles can be incredibly frustrating when progress feels impossible. When I was in this position, I made it my mission to find ways to overcome roadblocks and become a more effective problem solver. Through trial and error, I developed practical workarounds and strategies. Such experiences helped me gain new perspectives and a different approach to problem-solving. By analyzing my experiences and the techniques I took, these principles gradually became second nature to me. They became my go-to methods when faced with challenges and are integral to my success. Now, by sharing what I have learned in this book, I hope to help others become more creative problem solvers. With the immense benefits of this book, you will likely accomplish more than you ever thought possible.

To offer a fresh perspective on problem-solving, this book introduces four pillars. The book's first pillar focuses on understanding the problem, a critical aspect of problem-solving. As such, you will learn to analyze the issue thoroughly and gather relevant data. This will make it easier to articulate and decide on the best approach to resolving a problem. With a solid foundation in place, the second pillar offers various options and methodologies to strategize and develop the best solution to the problem.

Meanwhile, the third pillar involves selecting the best solution among multiple options. As such, it focuses on evaluating and prioritizing potential solutions, making a choice, and implementing the solution of choice. This approach helps to optimize the decision-making process, which is vital in resolving complex issues. Inevitably, problem-solving comes with limitations and challenges, as highlighted in the fourth pillar. These challenges can include a lack of clarity, bias, assumptions, and limited resources such as time and support. The fourth pillar is designed to help overcome these challenges and obstacles by introducing techniques and strategies to manage them.

At its core, this book aims to enhance your problem-solving abilities by helping you overcome inherent human biases in decision-making. Unfortunately, humans are prone to decision-making biases, leading to suboptimal outcomes. Yet, with the help of this book, you can strengthen your cognitive muscle to become a better problem-solver and a more successful person.

Developing an effective and straightforward method to solve challenges is vital for facing a big or small problem. Considering that, this book will provide a simple yet powerful process for identifying the problem. Likewise, it will make formulating well-thought-out solutions and implementing them effectively smoother. It not only improves the quality of your solutions. Yet, it also helps you take a systematic approach to tackling obstacles. Hence, this book is a must-read for anyone looking to sharpen their problem-solving abilities and take their life to the next level.

In conclusion, this book contains core problem-solving concepts and principles distilled into a straightforward, accessible form. Each chapter will teach you the different theories and techniques you can apply in any personal or collaborative setting. The methods and strategies you are about to read are proven to yield incredible results. Now, it is time to take action and become a more effective problem solver.

Chapter 1:
Problem-Solving Fundamentals

Are you ready to take your problem-solving skills to the next level? The ability to solve problems is crucial both in your professional and personal life. It involves identifying, analyzing, and overcoming challenges that impede your progress. Finding effective, efficient, and pragmatic solutions to problems requires a range of cognitive abilities. This chapter will cover everything you need to know about problem-solving, including its definition, significance, and ways to enhance your skills. Let us dive in and tackle those challenges together.

What Is Problem-Solving?

Throughout our lives, we face various daily problems that must be solved to move forward and achieve our goals. With the help of effective problem-solving, we can address issues and make sound choices that lead to success. That said, problem-solving is essential when dealing with personal or professional challenges.

Definition of Problem-Solving

When challenges arise, finding effective solutions through identification is what we call problem-solving. In other words, it is the ability to create solutions. A person who excels in problem-solving can identify the root cause of the problem and build an appropriate action plan. Not only does problem-solving involve addressing current issues, but it also entails devising lasting solutions that prevent potential future complications.

Becoming an effective problem solver requires critical thinking and decision-making skills. For instance, we must be able to evaluate the situation critically and make decisions that will have a positive impact. Critical thinking involves analyzing the problem from different perspectives and proposing appropriate solutions. Meanwhile, decision-making consists of evaluating the options available and selecting the best based on the situation's needs and requirements.

Aside from that, problem-solving requires other skills that help individuals approach challenges, including:

- **Creativity.** Generating new ideas and exploring solutions that may not be immediately apparent enables us to approach problems innovatively. Thus, it leads to more effective and efficient solutions.

- **Analytical Thinking.** Analyzing and interpreting data effectively help identify a problem's root cause and determine the best solution. Likewise, it allows us to approach problems systematically and make informed decisions based on data.

- **Open-mindedness.** Considering multiple perspectives without bias and exploring various angles contributes to finding the optimal solution to a problem.

- **Persistence.** Staying focused and resilient in the face of challenges and setbacks helps us to keep moving forward toward finding a solution. Hence, it lets us overcome obstacles and continue to explore new possibilities until a solution is found.

- **Collaboration.** Working effectively with others and leveraging their skills and perspectives is vital in solving complex problems collaboratively. For instance, it allows us to draw on diverse perspectives and knowledge, leading to more innovative and effective solutions.

There are three problem-solving approaches: *analytical, creative, and behavioral.*

- **Analytical approach.** Breaks down the problem into smaller pieces to identify the root cause and effect.

- **Creative approach.** Generates innovative solutions to solve the problem by thinking outside of the box.

- **Behavioral approach.** Considers how people are affected by the problem and creates solutions that benefit them.

These three approaches are essential as they offer different perspectives and problem-solving strategies. As such, the analytical approach helps to identify the underlying issue. Then the creative approach encourages new and innovative ideas. Meanwhile, the behavioral approach prioritizes the needs of the people affected by the problem. By combining these approaches, individuals and teams can create well-rounded solutions that benefit everyone involved.

As we develop our problem-solving ability, we foster creativity. Subsequently, it improves decision-making skills and leads to innovation.

It also boosts confidence and self-esteem, promotes teamwork, and enhances communication skills. Hence, problem-solving allows for the identification of weaknesses and improvements to be made.

Problem-Solving in Various Fields

Solid problem-solving skill is a common thread that runs through most successful individuals in any field. Regardless of one's specialization, the capacity to evaluate issues and offer solutions through problem-solving is instrumental in achieving our objectives. Additionally, this ability to approach problems systematically distinguishes successful individuals from those who struggle to find solutions.

Due to that, problem-solving is one of the most sought-after skills in different fields, including:

Business

In the business world, problem-solving skills are highly valued. Every day, business owners and executives face many challenges, such as finding ways to cut costs, increasing revenue, or mitigating risk. The ability to approach a problem creatively, analyze it, and develop viable solutions can determine whether a business thrives or fails. Strong problem-solving skills are also essential for those in sales, marketing, or customer service. For instance, businesses can improve customer loyalty and boost retention rates by identifying and addressing customer problems.

Education

Problem-solving skills are equally important in the field of education. As such, teachers have to deal with numerous problems that directly impact students' learning outcomes. These problems may include student behavior issues, declining enrollment, and inadequate resources. Identifying and developing strategies to address these issues will foster a supportive learning environment. Educators with strong problem-solving skills can anticipate and prevent challenges before they occur. Likewise, it will allow them to find innovative ways to improve student performance.

Meanwhile, problem-solving enables students to develop an analytical mindset and a systematic approach to learning. It enhances their critical thinking and decision-making skills, which are essential for academic success. As they engage in different courses and assignments that require problem-solving, students become more confident in expressing themselves. Besides that, they gain a more profound understanding of themselves and the world around them.

Science

Science relies heavily on problem-solving, making it an essential skill that cannot be underestimated. For instance, problem-solving is fundamental to inquiry-based learning, which involves asking questions, solving problems, and reflecting on the outcomes. Scientists have to deal with various complex problems, from choosing the right research methodology to selecting appropriate instruments. By analyzing these problems and using the scientific method, scientists can develop experimental designs that accurately measure the variables.

Furthermore, scientists must be able to combine creativity and critical thinking to form hypotheses, design experiments, and analyze data to obtain meaningful results. With effective problem-solving skills, scientists can overcome the challenges they face when attempting to advance their field. Thus, problem-solving helps them to develop new technologies and innovative solutions that can revolutionize the world.

Technology

Within the tech industry, problem-solving is vital as new and emerging technologies constantly present unique challenges. The intricate nature of technology often requires in-depth analysis and creative solutions to overcome obstacles that arise. Similarly, its fast-paced environment demands innovative solutions to complex issues.

Companies like Apple, Microsoft, and Amazon have reported that problem-solving is one of the key skills they look for in potential employees. As competition in the industry intensifies, these companies recognize that having employees with strong problem-solving abilities can give them an edge, making them more appealing to investors and customers who value efficient service.

Medicine

Considering patient history, symptoms, and other factors, healthcare providers must identify the problem and craft an effective treatment plan. In doing it, they must be detail-oriented, analytical, and quick thinkers to make accurate and efficient decisions. In fact, the medical breakthroughs we see today, such as treatments and medication, result from years of consistent problem-solving in the medical field.

Therefore, without it, treatments would not exist, and patients would not get the care they deserve.

Law

Lawyers are no strangers to problem-solving. For instance, they must assess complex situations and determine their clients' best action. Likewise, they need to be skilled in identifying the root cause of the issue, analyzing evidence, and crafting legal arguments. They also need to be persuasive, logical, and able to communicate clearly. Hence, lawyers who can solve legal problems time-sensitively are more likely to succeed in their careers.

As evident from the examples above, problem-solving is not just essential; it is vital for success in any demanding profession. People who can approach challenges with a problem-solving mindset tend to be more sought-after and benefit from job satisfaction and advancement opportunities.

Pillar 1: Understanding the Problem

When it comes to problem-solving, the first and arguably most integral step is understanding the problem. Without a clear understanding of the problem, it is impossible to develop effective solutions. That is where the first pillar of problem-solving comes in. This pillar is outlined to assist you in defining, analyzing, and gathering information about the challenge you are confronting. Likewise, it will explore the tools and techniques that can aid in this critical step of the problem-solving process. By gaining a deeper understanding of the problem, you can approach it more systematically and develop effective solutions that address the root cause.

Chapter 2:
Define the Problem

In the grand scheme of things, we all face problems of varying degrees of difficulty and complexity. Yet, the true test of our character lies in our ability to confront them head-on. However, tackling these challenges is not as simple as it seems. Before brainstorming solutions, you need to identify the problem's symptoms. Then, you must clarify its scope and develop a clear problem statement with specific objectives. Considering that, this chapter will explore problem framing and reframing techniques, data collection and analysis, and problem statement development. By the end of this chapter, you will have the tools to face any problem systematically.

Identify the Problem and Its Symptoms

Every organization must acknowledge that areas need improvement in pursuit of success. The path to uncovering these imperfections lies in the ability to discern the problem and its symptoms. Often, these symptoms are the manifestation of underlying problems. That said, it is essential to recognize and address them before they escalate.

Problem Identification

Identifying problems in the workplace is a bit like detective work, requiring a sharp eye to identify the telltale signs of the issues. For instance, if a lack of teamwork is holding you back, detecting the symptoms of this problem is essential in unlocking the key to their solution. By mastering the art of problem identification, you can uncover its root cause. Thus, allowing you to pave the way to a more effective workplace.

Feeling overwhelmed with endless tasks and responsibilities is a common problem for many in their personal lives. This frustrating state can appear in various forms, from incessant irritability to an inability to concentrate or a complete lack of motivation. Yet, it is necessary to determine these symptoms and delve into their source. Once the cause is pinpointed, the path to solutions like delegating tasks or creating a prioritization system becomes clear.

Moreover, low employee morale and high turnover rates are common problems that businesses face. The symptoms of low morale could include decreased productivity, absenteeism, and negativity towards team members or management. Then, high turnover rates could mean that staff feel undervalued, underpaid, or are experiencing a lack of career progression. Identifying these symptoms early on and addressing the issues causing them is essential to avoid losing valuable staff and maintaining a healthy work environment.

Failing to identify problems and their symptoms can negatively impact our lives. Likewise, misdiagnosis or ignoring symptoms may lead to more problems over time, and it may become challenging to resolve the issue. It can also lead to an imbalance in our personal and professional lives, affecting our health, happiness, and well-being.

The 4 Pillars of Problem-Solving

Problem Framing and Reframing

Problem framing involves analyzing a situation to determine the underlying problem accurately. This thinking method helps examine the problem from various angles to determine the root cause and understand the challenges that require resolution. In contrast, problem reframing involves redefining the problem to gain an objective, fresh perspective and identify alternative and better solutions. Hence, it lets us see the problem differently and develop unique ideas.

Let us take an example to illustrate this point. Suppose you are the CEO of a company experiencing declining sales. Likely, your initial instinct to solve the problem is by launching new marketing campaigns or expanding your product line. However, without a clear problem statement, you might waste resources. But by employing problem-framing and reframing techniques, you can uncover the real reasons behind the decline in sales and devise targeted solutions that are more likely to yield results.

Moreover, problem framing and reframing can lead to a host of additional benefits, including:

- **Improved Decision Making.** When faced with a problem, we naturally jump to finding a solution. However, this approach may only address surface-level issues rather than the underlying root problems. By framing and reframing the problem, we can approach the problem more thoroughly and make an informed decision based on the insights gained.

- **Enhanced Creativity and Innovation.** When reframing problems, we are forced to think creatively and outside the box. It, in turn, helps generate new, innovative ideas to identify potential opportunities we may have previously overlooked. Gaining a fresh perspective can help turn initial ideas into unique and exciting solutions.

- **Greater Collaboration and Teamwork.** When teams work together to achieve a common goal, they come with varying perspectives and viewpoints. Problem framing and reframing can assist in aligning these perspectives and goals, ultimately fostering greater teamwork and collaboration.

- **Increased Efficiency and Productivity.** With proper problem framing and reframing, problems can be more effectively addressed and resolved.

There are different methods you can use to approach problem framing and reframing, some of which include the following:

- **Boundary Examination.** Defining the boundaries of the problem and determining how different aspects affect it.

- **Challenging Assumption.** Assessing your assumptions and beliefs and identifying how they impact your approach to the problem.

- **Divergent Thinking.** Generating as many ideas as possible to come to a solution rather than relying on preconceived notions.

- **Analogies.** Comparing a current problem to a previous or entirely different problem to gain a fresh perspective.

By applying these concepts, we can become better problem solvers in our personal and professional lives, ultimately leading to greater success.

The 4 Pillars of Problem-Solving

Clarify the Problem and Its Scope

Understanding the problem you are dealing with is the first step in solving it. Clarifying the problem involves defining it and determining its scope. Defining the problem helps identify its characteristics while identifying the scope of the problem helps limit the problem's boundaries. Techniques for clarifying a problem include asking open-ended questions, brainstorming, conducting research, and identifying assumptions and biases.

Asking open-ended questions requires more than a *"yes"* or *"no"* answer. Examples of open-ended questions include *"How can we improve our customer service?"* or *"What are the different ways we can reduce our production costs?"* These questions help generate more ideas, allowing you to understand the problem better and explore possible solutions.

Brainstorming is another technique for clarifying the problem. This strategy involves gathering a group of people to generate ideas and possible solutions to the problem. Likewise, it allows for more perspectives to contribute, increasing the chance of identifying the right solution. Meanwhile, **conducting research** enables you to gather more information about the problem, which can help determine its cause and stakeholders. With this information, you can generate more options for solving the problem.

Besides that, **identifying and acknowledging our assumptions and biases** is essential because they can influence our decision-making process. Our assumptions are hold-beliefs about certain things that may or may not be true. Acting upon them without verifying their accuracy may lead to decisions based on false information. On the other hand, biases are our preferences, prejudices, and predispositions towards certain things or people, which can skew our perception and judgment. However, recognizing and addressing them ensure that we are working with accurate information and making decisions based on objective facts rather than subjective opinions or beliefs. Moreover, understanding our assumptions and biases can help us develop empathy and open-mindedness toward others, enabling us to communicate and collaborate more effectively.

Data Collection and Analysis Techniques

In problem-solving, data collection provides valuable information about the problem at hand. Without this information, creating a coherent picture of the problem and making informed decisions about how to proceed would be challenging.

Think of data collection as a flashlight that illuminates the path before you, making it easier to see what is ahead. Similarly, it allows you to gather information from various sources and perspectives, giving you a more holistic view of the situation. For instance, you can identify patterns, correlations, and trends that may not have been immediately apparent.

There are many data collection techniques, including:

- **Surveys.** Used to gather information from many people about a specific topic. Surveys can be conducted online or in person, depending on the target audience. The quantitative data from the respondents can be used to make informed decisions.
- **Interviews.** Involve one-on-one conversations with a person or a group of people related to the problem. This technique provides qualitative data, giving in-depth information on the problem.

- **Observation.** Employed to gather information about a specific behavior, process, or activity by observing and recording what is happening.

- **Secondary sources.** Information from existing resources, such as books, articles, and published reports. Gathering data through secondary sources provides background on the problem while saving you time and resources.

After collecting data, the next step is to analyze it. Data analysis involves examining the information gathered to identify patterns, relationships, and possible solutions.

When it comes to data analysis, different techniques can be applied, each serving a unique purpose. One such technique is **qualitative analysis**, which involves examining non-numerical data, such as interviews and observations, to identify patterns and themes. This method is advantageous when dealing with complex issues or small sample sizes.

Meanwhile, **quantitative analysis** involves examining numerical data, such as surveys, to determine statistical relationships between variables. This technique generates numerical data that can be used to draw conclusions and make informed decisions. Another technique commonly used is **statistical analysis**, which involves using statistical methods such as regression analysis to analyze the data more comprehensively, enabling more complex conclusions.

Finally, **root cause analysis** is a technique used to identify the underlying cause of a problem. It involves specifying the different factors related to the problem to uncover the root cause. By applying this technique, organizations can address the underlying problem rather than just treating the symptoms.

Hence, defining the issue's scope and collecting and analyzing relevant data allow us to modify our solutions in various cases.

Define the Problem Statement and Objectives

Every success or failure in life depends on a correct diagnosis of the problem, the formulation of clear objectives, and the ability to link them effectively. While identifying problems and setting objectives seems like a simple process, it requires a great deal of thought and skill. Otherwise, you risk a distorted understanding of what you are trying to achieve, which can end up leading to wasted effort, missed opportunities, and lost investments.

Problem Statement

At the heart of any successful problem-solving process lies a well-crafted problem statement. This problem statement is a brief but rich description of the issue. Likewise, it should be clear, concise, and able to answer the key questions: *What is the problem? Why does it matter? Who does it affect? Where and when does it occur?*

Defining the problem statement involves identifying the problem, describing its severity, and outlining its impact. Techniques for determining the problem statement include brainstorming. In brainstorming, think of all the possible problems that you are facing. Next, organize them by priority, and try to distill them down to a single statement. Another technique is creating a problem statement frame, which can provide structure and guidance. For instance, a problem statement frame might include the following elements: need, scope, cause, consequence, and criteria. Alternatively, use root cause analysis or SWOT (Strengths, Weaknesses, Opportunities, Threats) analysis.

These methods allow us to identify the root cause of the problem and get a 360-degree view of the situation.

Developing Objectives

After defining the problem statement, the next step is to develop measurable and achievable objectives. These objectives serve as a roadmap for solving the problem, providing specific and realistic targets to strive for. Setting clear objectives gives a clear picture of success and how to measure progress toward achieving it. Without objectives, losing sight of the end goal is likely. But with them, we can stay on track and focused, making steady progress toward the ultimate solution.

One effective technique for developing objectives is to use the SMART criteria. SMART stands for Specific, Measurable, Achievable, Relevant, and Time-bound. To establish objectives effectively, do the following steps:

1. **Identify the solution domain.** What area or field is relevant to problem-solving?
2. **Prioritize the objectives.** What are the most crucial and strategic objectives that align with the problem statement?
3. **Break down the objectives into sub-tasks.** What are the specific actions and deliverables that lead to achieving each objective?
4. **Define the metrics and indicators.** How will you measure the progress and success of each objective?
5. **Set deadlines and milestones.** When will each sub-task be completed, and when will each objective be achieved?

Another technique is to develop a decision matrix. With a decision matrix, you can compare options and prioritize your objectives based on their impact and feasibility.

Link the problem statement and objectives after defining and developing them. A clear link between your problem statement and objectives saves you time and resources on irrelevant activities. Likewise, it ensures that your objectives are aligned with your problem statement and contributes to the solution.

In visualizing the link between problem statements and objectives, use the cause-and-effect diagram or fishbone diagram. This diagram helps you identify the root cause of the problem and link it to your objectives. By doing so, you can ensure that your objectives are relevant to the problem and address its underlying causes. Another technique is to use the Gantt chart, which can help you visualize your objectives over time and track progress.

Recognizing a problem's symptoms and its root cause makes it possible to develop targeted solutions. Subsequently, problem framing and reframing can improve decision-making, enhance creativity and innovation, increase collaboration and teamwork, and increase efficiency and productivity. Techniques such as boundary examination, challenging assumption, divergent thinking, and analogies can be used to approach problem framing and reframing. Lastly, clarifying the problem involves defining it and determining its scope, which can be done by asking open-ended questions, brainstorming, conducting research, and identifying assumptions and biases.

Chapter 3:
Analyze the Problem

Starting a problem-solving process without a proper analysis phase can lead to wasted time and suboptimal outcomes. Before addressing the problem, taking a step back and carefully studying it is essential. In this chapter, we will delve into the fundamental processes of problem analysis, including identifying causal and contributing factors, performing root cause analysis, and more. By the end of this chapter, you will have the skills and knowledge necessary to conduct a thorough analysis of problems and identify the most effective solutions.

Identify Causal Factors

Causal factors are the underlying problems that result in the symptoms of the problem you are trying to solve. These underlying problems directly contribute to the problem you're trying to address. Suppose you have a leaky roof; the causal factor could be the lack of maintenance, the age of the roof, or poor quality material.

Identifying these causal factors of a problem helps prevent the recurrence of the problem. As such, remember to solve not only the symptoms but also the underlying causes. Without identifying causal factors, you can only solve the symptoms of the problem temporarily. Hence, it is likely that the problem will reappear. However, identifying causal factors allows the development of effective solutions that prevent the problem's recurrence.

Several methods can be employed to identify causal factors, including *brainstorming, root cause analysis, and the five whys technique*. Brainstorming involves generating several possible causes of the problem. Meanwhile, root cause analysis involves identifying the underlying cause by analyzing the factors contributing to the problem. Finally, the five whys technique involves asking five *"why"* questions to identify the root cause of the problem.

Besides that, when identifying causal factors, several factors must be considered. These include the *time frame of the problem, data availability and quality, system complexity, and bias and assumptions*. The time frame of the problem helps determine whether the issue is ongoing or a one-time event. Data availability and quality impact the accuracy of the analysis. System complexity considers how various factors interact and contribute to the problem. Then, bias and assumptions must be identified and avoided.

Likewise, common mistakes must be avoided when identifying causal factors to ensure an accurate and effective analysis. For instance, jumping to conclusions without considering all possible causes can lead to inaccurate results. Then, not considering all possible causes can also affect the analysis, leading to an incomplete understanding of the problem. Meanwhile, relying on assumptions or incomplete data can lead to skewed results that do not address the underlying issues. Finally, not involving key stakeholders in the analysis can lead to solutions that do not work in practice.

With these considerations in mind, you will be well on your way to mastering problem-solving.

Identify Contributing Factors

Delving deeper into the problem requires uncovering the underlying contributing factors that trigger or perpetuate the problem. These factors can stem from internal and external sources and often involve a combination of different elements. Pinpointing these factors is essential to grasping the problem's core, identifying the root cause, and crafting well-tailored solutions.

For instance, suppose a student struggles with poor grades in a particular subject. To identify the contributing factors, the student could ask themselves some questions. *Are they struggling to understand the material? Are they having difficulty with the way the teacher presents the information? Are they having trouble staying focused during class? Are they finding it hard to complete assignments on time?* By considering these questions, the student can identify the contributing factors causing their poor performance. Once identified, the student can take targeted action to address them and improve their academic performance.

Several methods can be used to identify contributing factors effectively. One technique is brainstorming, which helps generate a comprehensive list of potential factors contributing to the problem. Another method is to use a fishbone diagram to visualize the possible contributing factors. The fishbone diagram helps identify the root cause by breaking down the problem into different categories. Lastly, a failure mode and effects analysis (FMEA) can identify potential failure points in a system or process.

Across different fields, common contributing factors can be found that cause problems., such as:

- **Human error.** Even small mistakes can result in catastrophic failures or accidents. As humans, we make errors such as misjudgment or carelessness that can cause significant harm in fields such as healthcare, aviation, or manufacturing.

- **Communication breakdown.** Insufficient communication between different departments or team members can cause delays, misunderstandings, and loss of productivity. Likewise, it often leads to costly rework, missed deadlines, and incorrect results.

- **Inadequate training.** Lack of sufficient employee training can result in inefficient work or procedures, leading to errors and delays. Additionally, employees with inadequate training may lack the necessary skills to perform their duties, negatively affecting productivity.

- **Lack of resources.** A shortage of labor, material, or technology resources can hinder business operations and result in poor outcomes. Meanwhile, insufficient funding or poor resource management can put the organization at greater risk.

Aside from that, understanding the impact of these contributing factors is essential to long-term problem resolution. By assessing their impact, we can tackle the root causes of the issue rather than just the symptoms. There are two main techniques to evaluate the impact of contributing factors: *risk assessment and impact analysis.*

Risk assessment involves identifying risks associated with the problem and analyzing their likelihood and consequences. This technique is useful in situations where the problem has the potential to cause significant harm or loss. By assessing the risk, we can determine the feasibility of different solutions and select the one that minimizes the risks associated with the problem.

Meanwhile, impact analysis is a more in-depth assessment technique that analyzes the problem's impact on different areas such as people, processes, and finances. This approach is advantageous when the problem affects multiple areas and has far-reaching consequences. Moreover, it helps understand the scope of the problem and its potential impact on all aspects of the organization.

Both techniques are essential for a comprehensive analysis of the problem.

Conduct a Root Cause Analysis

Root cause analysis is a powerful problem-solving technique used by organizations to identify the underlying causes of a problem. Conducting a root cause analysis involves a systematic and thorough approach to understanding the problem, gathering information, and identifying the contributing factors. The goal of root cause analysis is to prevent the problem from reoccurring by addressing its underlying causes.

The following steps will help in conducting a root-cause analysis:

Identify the Problem

To conduct a successful root cause analysis, the first step is clearly defining the problem. This process involves understanding the problem and how it impacts the organization. Once you clearly understand the problem, gather information about it. As such, collect and analyze data to determine the problem's scope, magnitude, and frequency. Finally, determine the problem's impact to understand its financial, operational, or reputational effects.

Identify Possible Causes

Once you have identified the problem, the next step is identifying possible causes. First, brainstorm techniques to devise a list of all the potential causes of the problem. Remember to urge free thinking and avoid criticism during brainstorming to generate as many ideas as possible. After the list is created, narrow down the possible causes by considering the feasibility, impact, and frequency of each potential cause. At this stage, involve experts or stakeholders with experience and knowledge about the problem.

Another way to support possible causes is through data analysis. Analyzing data related to the problem helps identify patterns, trends, and correlations that point to potential causes. Data analysis can be done using statistical tools or software to identify possible outliers, trends, and other indicators that can support or refute a possible cause.

Analyze the Root Cause

After identifying possible causes, determine the root cause. Look for patterns or commonalities among the possible causes to determine which is most likely the root cause. Consider using tools such as:

Fishbone Diagram

By illustrating the potential causes and effects, this tool helps identify the root cause of problems. The diagram resembles a fish's skeleton. At the fish's head are the identified problems. Then, drawing bones extending from the head represents categories of potential causes such as people, processes, materials, environment, and equipment. The sub-causes are then attached to each bone. Thus, a fishbone diagram is a great tool for examining complex issues and identifying relationships between them.

5 Whys

A simple yet effective technique to determine the root cause of a problem. It involves asking "why" questions five times until the root cause is found. For example, *"Why did the machine malfunction?"* "Because the circuit board overheated." *"Why did the circuit board overheat?"* "Because the ventilation system was not working correctly." *"Why was not the ventilation system working correctly?"* "Because it had not been maintained properly." *"Why was it not maintained properly?"* "Because there was no scheduled maintenance program in place." By asking why five times, you can uncover possible causes, eliminate them, and ensure that you address the real issue.

Pareto Analysis

Focus on identifying problems or causes based on their frequency of occurrence. For instance, the sample chart below shows, in descending order, the various issues or potential causes why people fail their tests. The idea is to focus on the 20% of problems or causes contributing to 80% of the problem.

Fault Tree Analysis

A visual representation of all the possible causes and conditions contributing to the event. The tree is upside down, where the *"fault"* is at the top, and the branches represent the potential causes. Each factor that could contribute to the event is analyzed and quantified. After that, an assessment is made to identify which factors have the highest likelihood of causing the problem.

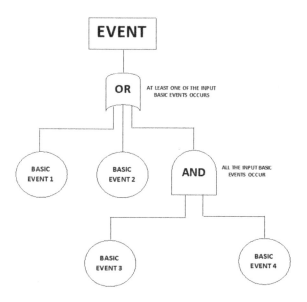

Process Mapping

Represents the process through visuals to understand how it works and identify areas for improvement.

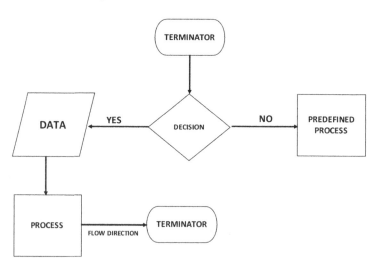

The 4 Pillars of Problem-Solving

Effective problem-solving requires a thorough analytical phase that examines the problem and its underlying causes. Skipping this phase can result in inefficient solutions and a waste of time. To ensure a successful outcome, it is essential to identify the causal and contributing components and include all relevant parties if necessary. Meticulous planning, creative solutions, and detecting the underlying cause are vital for successful problem-solving. Contributing variables must also be treated to relieve symptoms and speed up the process, and the interdependence of various components must be considered. Overall, a careful and analytical approach is crucial for effective problem-solving.

Chapter 4:
Gathering Information

Gathering information is the cornerstone of successful problem-solving, paving the way for innovative solutions and strategic decision-making. Moreover, this process involves learning different research methods and factors to consider.

Conduct Research

Research involves systematically investigating a subject or problem for new knowledge or insights. For problem-solving purposes, research means gathering information and data to develop a deep understanding of the situation, including its causes, effects, and potential solutions. Moreover, it provides a foundation for decision-making by empirical evidence, identifying patterns and gaps, sorting through complex issues, and uncovering assumptions.

There are several reasons why conducting research is crucial in the problem-solving process. First, research helps identify the root cause of the problem. Without a deep understanding of the issue, any proposed solution will be temporary. The second reason is to uncover potential solutions. Research can provide evidence to support or dismiss proposed solutions, paving the way for more informed decision-making. Third, research provides context. It allows us to understand how the problem relates to bigger issues, such as industry trends, new technologies, or social dynamics. Lastly, it helps to mitigate risks and uncertainties. By identifying potential problems, decision-makers can better anticipate obstacles and adjust their strategies accordingly.

There are different types of research methods, such as:

Surveys and Interviews

To start with, surveys and interviews are two methods of collecting data from people with a specific objective in mind. Surveys are usually written questions that the respondents fill out. Meanwhile, interviews are conducted in person to gather insights into a particular topic or subject.

Advantages

The major advantage of surveys is that they can be easily distributed to a large group of people and provide quantitative data. For instance, surveys can be conducted online, through mail, or in person. It is also a low-cost method for collecting a large amount of data.

On the other hand, interviews provide qualitative data. As such, interviews give insights into the participant's opinions, thoughts, and perspectives on a specific topic. Thus, it enables researchers to dig deeper and ask for follow-ups to understand the meaning behind the responses.

Disadvantages

While surveys are useful for collecting data, remember that they may not provide comprehensive information. Likewise, the respondent may only provide superficial answers without providing in-depth insights.

There is also a possibility of bias in surveys as the respondent's experience and opinions can influence the answers.

Meanwhile, the disadvantage of interviews is that it is difficult to analyze the data obtained. The responses can also be subjective and biased based on the interviewer's experience, knowledge, and opinions.

To avoid the disadvantages of surveys and interviews, you may:

- **Use open-ended questions.** Instead of asking closed-ended questions, try using open-ended questions that allow the respondent to give detailed and thoughtful answers. This approach encourages respondents to provide more comprehensive information, and the data collected is less likely to be superficial.

- **Offer anonymity.** Providing anonymity in surveys can help reduce bias and encourage respondents to be more honest and open in their answers. In interviews, this can be achieved by having a neutral party conduct the interview or by providing a safe and private environment.

- **Utilize a diverse sample.** To avoid bias, include a diverse group of respondents representing the studied population. This way, you ensure that the data collected is representative of the entire population and not just one particular group.

- **Triangulate data.** To ensure the data's accuracy and validity, use multiple data collection methods such as surveys, interviews, observations, and experiments. Consequently, it will help to cross-check the data and reduces the likelihood of biased data.

Hence, choose a survey for collecting data from a large and diverse group. Alternatively, go for an interview to gather in-depth and nuanced information from a smaller and specific population.

Observations, Experiments, and Simulations

The process of gathering data through visual, auditory, or tactile means is called **observation**. This empirical method collects information on an event, phenomenon, or object. This method is frequently used in scientific research to determine specific characteristics of a subject under study. For instance, in medical research, observations can help to monitor the progress of a patient's condition over time, such as using MRI scans to monitor the progression of brain tumors. Besides that, observation is non-invasive, cost-effective, and can provide detailed and accurate information.

Meanwhile, **experiments** are the systematic process of testing a hypothesis using controlled conditions. By varying certain variables and observing the impact on a response, experiments can provide evidence for causality. In business and marketing, experiments can be run to determine the most effective marketing channels, user experience testing, and optimizing website design. Although experiments may require considerable time and funding, the ability to control for different variables makes it a powerful tool to test hypotheses, identify causality, and provide strong evidence for decision-making.

Lastly, **simulations** are virtual models that imitate real-world scenarios in a controlled environment. They enable professionals to recreate complex interactions and behaviors that would be difficult or near-impossible to achieve in practical settings. Simulations can also test various scenarios, change variables to see the effect, and predict how things could play out. In medicine, simulations are used to train learners in realistic scenarios, such as patient care, surgical procedures, or anesthesia management.

Advantages

One significant advantage of using observations, experiments, and simulations is that each provides a perspective on the subject under study. Observations offer detailed and specific information on the topic. Then, experiments allow scientists to test hypotheses and provide empirical evidence. Besides that, simulations help individuals conceptualize and understand the implications of their actions in complex situations. Additionally, these methods are low-risk, cost-effective, and can provide valuable and accurate data, making them ideal for professionals in various fields.

Disadvantages

While each of the three methods holds value, there are also potential drawbacks. For instance, observations have a moderate risk of bias as the observer's interpretation plays a significant role in recorded observations. Conversely, experiments may not be fully generalizable to real-world scenarios as they are conducted in artificial environments, which may not translate accurately to the real world. Likewise, simulations can provide accurate information, but they are only as good as the data input, meaning inaccurate data could result in poor decisions.

Maximize the benefits of every method by following these simple steps to avoid any potential pitfalls.

- **To minimize observation bias:** Use a structured observation plan and have multiple observers cross-check the results.

- **To increase the generalizability of experiments:** Try to replicate real-world scenarios as much as possible and use a representative sample of participants.

- **To ensure the accuracy of simulations:** Use high-quality and relevant data inputs, and validate the results against real-world data whenever possible.

Aside from that, being mindful of the potential pitfalls and limitations of each can improve their efficacy.

Gather Data

To solve problems, make informed decisions, and plan effectively, data acquisition is crucial. Various methods can be used to collect data, such as evaluating information from databases and records, monitoring social media and online analytics, conducting surveys, interviewing individuals, and observing relevant situations.

Collecting and Analyzing Data From Databases and Records

To obtain and evaluate data, you can retrieve information from public records, business databases, and other digital archives. This type of data collection is advantageous when collecting primary data is impossible or when there is a large amount of data. Likewise, market analysis, consumer data analysis, demographic data analysis, and financial analysis all benefit from this approach.

There are several phases to consider to gather and analyze data from databases and records. The first phase involves *identifying appropriate sources* to collect the data necessary for the study. After collecting the data from various sources, it must be *organized* to facilitate easy evaluation. Then, the third phase involves *cleaning the data* to eliminate any discrepancies, duplicates, or errors that might compromise the accuracy of the analysis. In the fourth phase, statistical techniques such as *clustering, regression, and correlation analysis* are used to evaluate the data and identify any patterns, trends, or correlations.

Ultimately, the analysis results are used to make informed judgments and decisions.

Monitoring Social Media and Web Analytics

For businesses to remain competitive in the modern digital world monitoring social media and online analytics is necessary. Social media platforms such as Facebook, Twitter, Instagram, and LinkedIn, offer a wealth of information on consumer behavior, industry trends, and brand perception. Additionally, web analytics platforms like Google Analytics provide user interaction, traffic, and conversion rates data. By monitoring these platforms, businesses can gain insights into their target audiences, identify emerging trends, and evaluate the success of their marketing initiatives.

To ensure the effectiveness of a business's online presence, follow several steps in this process. First, find the most appropriate social media platforms and web analytics tools. For instance, consider if your chosen platform offers precise metrics for your type of company. Second, install tracking codes or pixels on your website and social media pages, which may require technical knowledge. The third step involves configuring analytics tools to track user engagement, traffic, and conversion rates. Then the fourth and final step is analyzing the collected data using statistical methods. These methods include *cohort analysis, A/B testing, or funnel analysis* to identify areas for improvement and make data-driven decisions.

For example, by analyzing a high bounce rate, a company can identify areas for website improvement, such as adjusting the layout, providing more information, and making call-to-action icons more visible. Improving these areas can increase user engagement and conversion rates.

Thus, monitoring web analytics and social media is essential for businesses to collect accurate data, gain valuable insights, and optimize their online presence to increase user engagement and conversion rates.

Effective problem-solving relies on conducting research. To ensure quality research, various tools are available for data collection, including surveys, interviews, observations, experiments, and simulations. After data collection, a thorough analysis is necessary to consider potential limitations or biases that may affect the findings. In cases where primary data collection is impossible, or the data is extensive, retrieving information from databases and records can be beneficial. Furthermore, social media and online analytics provide valuable insights into consumer behavior, industry trends, and brand perception. Thus, businesses can evaluate and refine their marketing success.

Pillar 2: Strategize

Three crucial topics are covered in this pillar: *flow charts and diagrams, SWOT analysis, and Six Sigma methodology.* Flow charts and diagrams enable the visualization of processes and identify areas of improvement. Subsequently, SWOT analysis helps identify a business's strengths, weaknesses, opportunities, and threats. The Sigma methodology is a data-driven approach to improving business operations. These topics will be a game-changer in your problem-solving process.

Chapter 5:
Flow Charts & Diagrams

Sometimes, there are complex processes or strategies that we may be struggling to make sense of it all. In such cases, various tools are used to help us simplify and understand the information. One such tool is the flowchart and diagram, which can visually represent a process or strategy, making it easier to comprehend and communicate.

Definition and Importance

Indispensable in several industries, including software development, business, engineering, and education, diagrams and flowcharts allow for the visualization of intricate systems, pattern recognition, and data analysis.

Flowcharts are graphical representations that provide a visual overview of a process or system. They consist of a series of interconnected symbols that represent different elements of the process. Meanwhile, **diagrams** are graphical representations used to describe various concepts and relationships between them.

Moreover, these tools offer a range of benefits. In fact, their use in the business world has become increasingly prevalent in recent years due to their ability to save time, reduce inefficiencies, and enhance team collaboration. Many businesses use flowcharts and diagrams to map out processes, troubleshoot issues, and identify areas of improvement. Educators also use these tools to represent complex theories or ideas and discuss them with their students.

Types of Flowcharts and Diagrams

Different types of flowcharts and diagrams serve various purposes. Some of the most common types of flowcharts include:

Process Flowcharts

A process flowchart is a graphic representation of steps and activities that define a process or workflow. They detail the inputs, outputs, decision points, and flow of processes. Likewise, they serve as an overview of a process, making it easier for people to understand the various components of the process.

Besides that, process flowcharts offer numerous benefits to businesses and organizations, such as:

- **Improved Understanding of the Process.** A well-defined process flowchart helps understand how each process fits into the broader picture.

- **Identification of Bottlenecks and Process Improvements.** From the flowchart, we can verify where delays occur and why. With this information, we can find possible solutions to improve the process, making it more efficient and cost-effective.

- **Communication and Collaboration.** Provide a common language to discuss and communicate on a particular process.

Thus, it helps eliminate miscommunication or misunderstandings, reducing the chance of errors or confusion.

- **Training and Onboarding.** Act as a standard reference guide for those unfamiliar with certain processes. This way, employees are more likely to learn quickly and work efficiently, increasing productivity.

- **Compliance and Audit.** Serve as evidence that the process complies with regulations and standards that may apply to a particular industry or business. The flowchart makes it easier for auditors to assess that the business follows procedures and rules for a particular process.

In creating a process flowchart, it is essential to understand the various components that make up the diagram. A process flowchart consists of several components, which include:

- **Start and End Points.** Circles usually express the beginning and end of a process.

- **Decision Points.** Represented by diamond shapes, decision points illustrate the options available at a particular step in a process.

- **Process Steps.** These are simple rectangles that represent individual steps in the process.

- **Flow Arrows.** Arrows represent the sequential flow of the process and keep the diagram organized.

- **Input and Output.** These are essential aspects of a process flowchart as they highlight the data that goes into and comes out of a process.

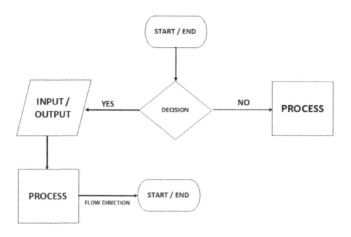

When creating a process flowchart, follow these essential steps to make it impactful.

Determine the Purpose and Scope

Clarify why you need a process flowchart and what process to document. *Do you want to identify bottlenecks, simplify tasks, or train new employees? Do you want to map the entire process or focus on a specific activity?* The purpose and scope will guide you in deciding what information to include in the flowchart.

Identify the Process

Once you have defined the purpose and scope, identify the process you want to document. *What is the starting point? What are the inputs and outputs? Who are the responsible parties? What are the possible outcomes?* Brainstorm with your team or subject matter experts to ensure you include all the essential aspects of the process.

The 4 Pillars of Problem-Solving

Collect and Organize Information

Gather all the information you need to create the flowchart. Either review existing documentation, interview stakeholders, observe the process, or use other data-gathering techniques. Then, organize the data into a logical structure that reflects the sequence of steps.

Determine the Sequence of Steps

Once you have the data, determine the order of the steps in the process. Use process mapping techniques or other methods to clarify the flows and interactions between activities.

Draft the Flowchart

With the sequence of steps established, create a draft of the flowchart. Use commonly recognized symbols, such as circles for states, diamonds for decisions, arrows for direction, and others. Then, draft the flowchart using a software tool or drawing by hand.

Review and Refine

After completing the flowchart, review it for accuracy and completeness. Verify if it meets its intended purpose and scope. Ensure that you identify and correct any errors or inconsistencies that may arise. Finally, refine the flowchart to make it clear and easy to understand by all stakeholders.

Furthermore, in making the process flowchart, be aware of these common mistakes:

- **Overcomplicating the Flowchart.** Avoid adding too many details, including information that is not relevant, or using complicated symbols. Keep the flowchart simple and clear, focusing on the essential aspects of the process.

- **Lack of Clarity.** Ensure the flowchart is easy to read, with clear labels, well-defined shapes, and concise descriptions. Use standard fonts, colors, and sizes that are readable from a distance. Test the flowchart with potential users to assess its clarity.

- **Failure to Involve Stakeholders.** Flowcharts are not created in a vacuum. Involve subject matter experts, process owners, and other stakeholders in the creation process to ensure that the flowchart reflects their perspectives and feedback.

- **Incomplete or Inaccurate Information.** Ensure that the data used to create the flowchart is accurate, up-to-date, and comprehensive. Verify the data with the sources and update the flowchart as needed.

- **Ignoring Revisions and Updates.** Keep your flowchart up-to-date, review it regularly, and revise it when necessary. Processes change over time, and the flowchart should reflect those changes to be useful.

Creating an effective process flowchart requires a disciplined approach and attention to detail. As such, ensure that your flowchart helps you to understand, communicate, and improve your processes. Lastly, avoid the aftermentioned common mistakes to ensure that your flowchart is accurate, clear, and useful.

Swimlane Diagrams

In depicting organizational processes and interactions, swimlane diagrams or cross-functional flowcharts are commonly used. Particularly, this flowchart helps identify bottlenecks, inefficiencies, and areas for improvement.

There are two main types of swimlane diagrams: *horizontal and vertical.* The **horizontal diagram** represents processes that flow from left to right. Typically, each lane represents a different department or role. In contrast, the **vertical diagram** flows from top to bottom, conveying each lane with a different process stage.

Swimlane diagrams have five main components, such as:

1. **Swimlanes.** Columns or rows in the diagram represent the different individuals or teams involved in the process. Typically, swimlanes are labeled at the top or side with the name of the person or department involved. As such, swimlanes help clarify who is responsible for each stage of the process.

2. **Processes.** Steps involved in completing the task or achieving the goal of the diagram. The processes are usually represented by rectangles in swimlane diagrams and are labeled with a short activity description.

3. **Decisions.** Diamonds represent decisions in swimlane diagrams. The purpose of including the decisions is to indicate the different options in the process that the decision maker has.

4. **Start and End Points.** Ovals illustrate the start and end points in swimlane diagrams. The start and end points are significant,

indicating where the diagram begins and ends. They also clarify the boundaries of the process represented in the diagram.

5. **Connectors.** The arrows that connect the different shapes and indicate the flow of the process. For instance, connectors help show the relationship between the diagram's various stages, decisions, swimlanes, and endpoints.

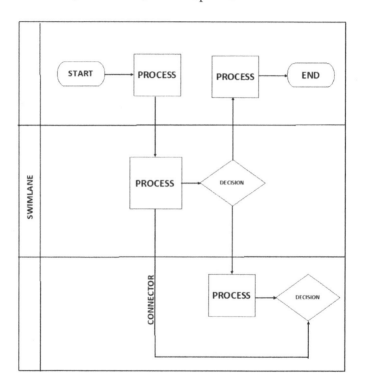

In ensuring that your swimlane diagram is effective, remember to:

Identify the Process

The first step in creating a swimlane diagram is to identify the process you want to represent visually. Once you have identified the process, you can map it out. Identifying the process is necessary because it will inform the design of the diagram and the swimlanes.

Determine the Swimlanes

Once you have identified the process, the next step is to determine the swimlanes. These swimlanes represent different departments or roles involved in the process and help visually organize the diagram. An effective way to determine the swimlanes is to consult with departmental coordinators or staff.

Add Processes and Decisions

After determining the swimlanes, add processes and decisions to the diagram. Adding these elements to the swimlane diagram will help clarify the process, making it more understandable and efficient.

Include Start and End Points

A start point marks the beginning of the process, while the endpoint marks the end. Including these points is essential as they provide closure to the process and ensure that everyone understands precisely when the process ends.

Connect the Components

The final step to creating the swimlane diagram is to connect the components. Using arrows, connect the shapes representing the processes and decisions. These arrows help to visualize the flow of the process. When connecting the components, ensure that the arrows follow the correct sequence.

Moreover, swimlanes come with limitations, such as:

Complexity

One of the limitations of swimlane diagrams is that they can become complex, particularly for processes with many steps. To address this limitation, keeping the swimlane diagram as simple as possible is essential. Hence, only include essential processes and decisions to avoid overwhelming your audience.

Time-Consuming

Creating swimlane diagrams can be time-consuming, especially for complex processes. One way to overcome this limitation is to use software tools to automate the creation of swimlane diagrams. As such, choose various software tools that save you time and effort.

Limited Scope

Swimlane diagrams have a limited scope and may not be suitable for some processes. For example, they may not be ideal for processes that involve complex data flows and multiple inputs and outputs. In such cases, use alternative tools like process flowcharts.

Lack of Flexibility

While swimlane is effective for depicting linear processes, it can be restrictive for processes that are not linear. To overcome this limitation, use swimlane diagrams with other tools, such as flowcharts or process maps.

Hence, swimlane diagrams are a powerful tool for illustrating processes and workflows in business. For instance, they help identify inefficiencies and improve your processes by clearly representing the work performed. However, swimlane diagrams have limitations, such as complexity, time-consuming, limited scope, and lack of flexibility.

By understanding these limitations, you can overcome them and create swimlane diagrams that are effective and efficient.

Cause-and-Effect Diagrams

Diagrams, such as cause-and-effect diagrams or fishbone diagrams, help pinpoint a problem's causes. Moreover, these diagrams can help teams work more efficiently, minimize errors, and reduce costs. By breaking down the problem into its root causes, you can prevent future issues from occurring. Applying cause-and-effect diagrams can also help you communicate with your team more effectively. For instance, they provide a clear framework for discussing potential problems, which can lead to more effective collaboration and constructive feedback.

A fishbone diagram resembles a fish's skeleton, where the head represents the problem. Subsequently, the bones symbolize the potential causes. Besides that, it usually has four main branches that help identify the main cause categories. These are *people, processes, equipment, and materials.* **People** are the human resources involved in the problem and can refer to employees or customers. **Processes** cover all the procedures involved in the situation, starting from the beginning of the problem until its resolution. Then, **equipment** refers to all the physical tools used, including technology. Meanwhile, **materials** include all elements involved in the problem, including raw materials and finished products.

Under each of the four main categories are additional sub-branches that further break down the details of the cause-and-effect relationships. Let us take *"processes"* as an example. Under this category, you can include communication issues, inadequate training, or inefficient workflow. Then, you can also further drill down into the causes by creating sub-sub-branches under each category. For instance, inadequate communication can lead to misunderstandings, or an absence of information can impede progress.

To create a clear and effective cause-and-effect diagram, do the following:

Identify the Problem

Gather customer and employee feedback, or review a performance metric that does not meet the organization's expectations. Ensure that the problem you identify is specific and clear rather than too broad or vague.

Determine the Main Categories of Causes

These categories can be identified by brainstorming with a team, analyzing data, or reviewing business processes. A maximum of six categories is recommended as this helps to simplify the diagram and keep it focused.

Brainstorm and List Possible Causes

Involve the team in the brainstorming process as different perspectives can help to identify unique causes, and a diverse team can help to inspire creativity.

Add Sub-Branches to Each Category

Further explore and list additional possible causes. The sub-branches may include organizational culture, people, processes, policies, technology, or external factors such as the economy or competition.

The 4 Pillars of Problem-Solving

Analyze and Evaluate the Causes

Determine the level of impact each cause has and prioritize the top three causes that have the most significant impact on the problem. This step will help identify the problem's root cause and develop a viable solution.

While making a fishbone diagram, remember to use clear and concise language. Avoid technical terms that others might not understand. Likewise, avoid jumping to conclusions. For instance, it is easy to assume what is causing the problem, but it is better to list all possible causes before concluding. Other than that, consider multiple perspectives. Discuss the issue with colleagues or other professionals who have different viewpoints. Finally, update and revise the diagram as needed. Sometimes, after conducting further analysis, you might find a missing cause that needs to be added. Make sure to update the diagram to reflect the latest information.

Mastering this tool allows you to identify the root cause of an issue. Likewise, it makes it possible to identify areas where processes or systems might be changed, leading to a more efficient and productive organization.

Mind Maps

The organization and structure of ideas are fundamental benefits of mind maps. Instead of a linear and restrictive approach, mind maps are structured around a central idea and use branches to organize related information. In this approach, there is a more natural and fluid way of organizing information, making it easier to see linkages and connections between ideas. Thus, ideas can be developed more structured, leading to better understanding and retention.

Memory retention and recall are also improved using mind maps. The visual and spatial nature of mind mapping aids in remembering information, as the mind associates images and colors with key points. In fact, studies have shown that visual learning improves memory more than text-based learning. Additionally, using keywords and images in mind maps ensure that important information is readily accessible. This ability to recall information quickly makes mind maps an excellent exam preparation and revision tool.

Creativity and idea generation are other benefits of mind maps. The non-linear and associative nature of mind mapping opens up new pathways for thinking and can lead to new and innovative ideas. Exploring different tangents and branches sparks creativity that might not have been possible with traditional brainstorming methods. Mind maps are also great for creative professionals, such as writers, designers, and artists, who must generate new ideas and explore paths.

Moreover, visual learning and understanding are enhanced with mind maps. For instance, the combination of colors, images, keywords, and text can represent complex information in a way that is visually engaging and stimulating. Furthermore, visualizing the relationships between concepts can make understanding abstract and complex topics easier.

Subsequently, the component of a mind map is the following:

Central Idea or Topic

The central idea or topic of a mind map is the main idea we want to convey through the map. For instance, it is the core of the mind map and typically occupies the center of the map. Likewise, it is the focal point of all the branches, sub-branches, and keywords connected to it. Remember, a central idea or topic should be articulated precisely for a clear statement.

The 4 Pillars of Problem-Solving

Branches

Branches in a mind map are the primary categories or themes. As such, they radiate from the central idea and represent the main supporting points. Think of them as the chapters of a book that support the central theme. Each branch needs to be clearly labeled to avoid confusion. Furthermore, it is recommended that each branch should contain only one keyword. Doing this makes it easier to understand, read, and follow.

Sub-branches

Detailed extensions of the branches in the mind map. Generally, they should be placed under a specific branch. They are used to delve deeper into the information associated with a branch and provide more ideas for its support. Sub-branches can also have sub-branches themselves, creating a hierarchical structure. Yet, keep the sub-branches connected with the central idea and the respective branches.

Keywords

Often, keywords are the most crucial component of a mind map as it helps in quick comprehension. These words and phrases encapsulate the mind map's main points, sub-points, and themes. Likewise, it succinctly conveys a lot of information and helps in quick recall. It is necessary to be concise while choosing the keywords. Generally, having no more than six keywords per branch is recommended, each one being a one-word descriptor.

Here is what it would look like, using Personal Development as its central idea.

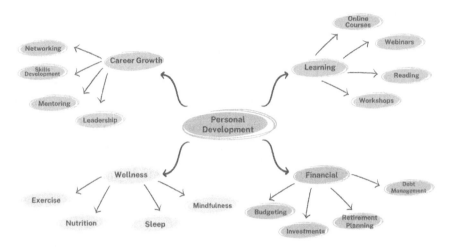

Images

Adding images to the mind map can make it more engaging and help retention. Keep images relevant to the central idea and the respective branches when choosing images. Images should also be used to supplement information, not distract or dominate.

When making a mind map, remember the following steps:

1. **Choose a Central Idea or Topic.** Should be in the middle of the page and written in bold or larger font. The purpose of this step is to focus your mind on the core of the project.

2. **Create Branches and Sub-Branches.** These branches and sub-branches represent different categories or subtopics of the project. For instance, if your central idea or topic is *'market analysis,'* create sub-branches, such as *'product analysis,' 'competitive analysis,' 'pricing analysis,'* and so on.

3. **Add Keywords and Images.** Once you have created the branches and sub-branches, you can add keywords and images.

Adding these elements makes recalling the information you have brainstormed easy.

4. **Use Color and Symbols.** Different colors or symbols can help you differentiate between branches and sub-branches and create a hierarchy of importance. For instance, if blue represents one category and red another, it would be easy to distinguish them within your mind map.

5. **Review and Revise.** Check if your mind map represents the entirety of your project logically. Yet, rearrange your mind map if it looks cluttered or does not flow well. Also, you can check if you have missed any essential details or connections. Each time you review and revise your mind map, you gain new insights and ideas, making your project richer and more effective.

Although mind mapping is an effective tool, it has some limitations and considerations you must know. For instance, mind mapping may not be effective for those who are not pleased with creating visuals or prefer linear outlines. It also may not work for those who have limited space or time. Furthermore, mind mapping is not a substitute for research or critical thinking; it is a tool to aid brainstorming. However, there are ways to overcome these limitations and considerations. For example, you can use lists or bullet points if you struggle with visual imagery. Subsequently, if you have limited space, create a digital mind map through different digital platforms.

Thus, mind mapping is an ingenious tool for anyone who wants to improve their brainstorming process. Similarly, it should be a part of every professional, executive, business owner's, and academic's toolkit.

Decision Trees

In predicting outcomes based on variables, decision trees are commonly used. This representation consists of nodes representing the decisions, branches illustrating the different outcomes, and leaves portraying the result. Decision trees are also popular in data analysis, especially in machine learning.

Furthermore, decision trees are built by recursively splitting the data based on the variables that create the best separation between the outcomes. The goal is to create a model that can accurately predict outcomes based on new input data. By splitting the data into different branches based on the variables, the decision tree establishes rules that can be followed to make predictions.

There are a variety of applications for decision trees, including:

- **Credit Risk Analysis.** Based on customer financial data, decision trees predict the probability of default or non-payment of loans.

- **Medical Diagnosis.** Used in medical diagnosis to predict the probability of disease based on various patient parameters.

- **Customer Segmentation.** Segment customers based on their buying behavior, preferences, and demographics.

- **Fraud Detection.** Utilized to detect fraudulent activities based on transaction patterns and other variables.

Aside from their versatility in various applications, decision trees offer several advantages over other machine learning algorithms. First, decision trees are easy to understand and interpret. For instance, they provide a clear and intuitive visual representation of the decision-making process. Hence, it makes it easy for non-technical stakeholders to understand the outcomes of the analysis. Second, decision trees can handle both categorical and numerical data. Categorical data includes variables such as gender or product category, while numerical data include age or income level variables.

Moreover, decision trees can handle non-linear relationships. This means they can identify complex relationships between variables in the data that may not be immediately apparent. For example, a decision tree can determine that customers who purchased product A and live in a certain geographic area are likelier to buy product B, even if there is no direct correlation between the two variables.

Likewise, there are various types of decision trees available, depending on the nature of the problem, industry, domain, and application:

- **Classification Trees.** A classification tree is used to classify a set of variables based on a pre-defined set of classes or categories. It is used in pattern recognition, data mining, prediction, and other critical applications.

- **Regression Trees.** Used to model continuous variables, such as measuring the dependent variable's value based on one or more independent variables. As such, it is used in cost analysis, pricing models, and other critical areas.

- **Cost-Sensitive Trees.** Show the cost associated with each possible decision outcome to help make more informed choices. Typically, it is used in industries with economic implications, such as healthcare and finance.

- **Ensemble Trees.** Combine multiple decision trees to create a more powerful and accurate model.

Subsequently, decisions trees have the following components:

- **Root Node.** Starting point of the decision tree represents the initial condition or state of the decision problem.

- **Decision Node.** Reflects a choice or decision operation to be taken. Once you have a decision node, you must have at least two potential outcomes *(usually yes/no or true/false)*.

- **Chance Node.** Denotes an event or circumstance that has the potential to happen and has an associated probability.

- **Leaf Node.** Represents the result or outcome of a decision. Once you arrive at a leaf node, the decision-making process is over. The resulting value of the leaf node is the final output or result of the decision-making process.

The 4 Pillars of Problem-Solving

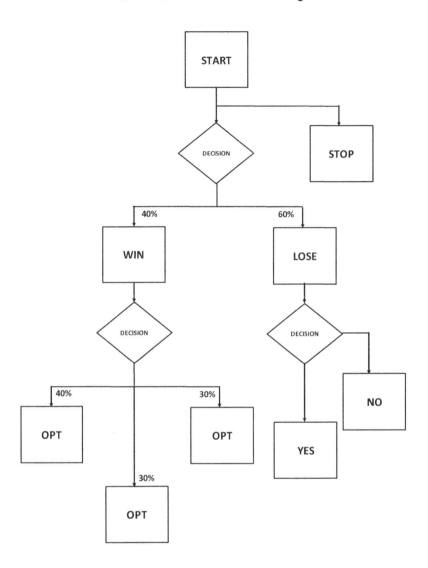

Here are some steps for creating a decision tree:

Data Preparation

Before building the decision tree, it is crucial to prepare the data. The data should be clean, and any missing values should be replaced appropriately through imputation. Also, the data must be split into training and testing sets. The training dataset is used to build the decision tree. Meanwhile, the testing set measures the model's accuracy using metrics.

Tree Building Algorithms

Different algorithms for building decision trees exist, such as ID3, C4.5, and CART. The **ID3** algorithm selects variables with the most information gain, while the **C4.5** selects variables based on their gain ratio. **CART**, on the other hand, employs the Gini index. All these algorithms have strengths and weaknesses, and it is paramount to assess them to choose the one that suits your needs.

Tree Pruning

Pruning is crucial in decision trees because it helps to reduce the complexity of the tree and, in turn, improves its performance. There are several ways to do pruning, such as reduced error pruning, cost complexity pruning, and least absolute shrinkage and selection operator (LASSO) pruning. **Reduced error pruning** employs the validation dataset to prune unnecessary nodes from the tree. Conversely, **cost complexity pruning** adds a cost parameter to the tree and prunes nodes with a higher cost. Then, **LASSO pruning** employs L1 regularization to reduce the number of features while increasing the accuracy of the tree.

Despite the effectiveness of decision trees, they have their limitations, which include the tendency to overfit the data, bias towards variables with more levels, sensitivity to small data variations, and difficulty handling continuous variables. Overfitting occurs when the tree is too complex and closely fits the training dataset, leading to poor performance on new data. To overcome overfitting, we can employ pruning.

Bias towards variables with more levels can be mitigated by limiting the number of levels each variable can have. Sensitivity to small data variations can be countered using random forests instead of a single decision tree. Finally, difficulties in handling continuous variables can be solved by grouping the data into categories or using regression trees.

Gantt Charts

Particularly, a Gantt chart is helpful in project management because it provides an overview of the entire project. It allows the team to organize and prioritize tasks and assign resources to each project phase. The chart visually illustrates the tasks' sequence and dependencies, so everyone involved can know when each task is expected to start and end. Thus, it is easier for the team to communicate, share ideas and make adjustments when necessary, ensuring the project stays on time, within budget, and meets its goals.

Gantt charts offer many benefits, including the fact that it helps the project team to organize and monitor the project schedule. Everyone on the team knows who handles each task and when each task is expected to begin and complete. By keeping everyone informed, Gantt charts can also help prevent project delays, miscommunications, and errors.

Another advantage of using Gantt charts is that it allows the project team to track its progress. Since every task has a predetermined duration, it is easy to follow if it is behind, on, or ahead of schedule since its time frame can be tracked at any time in the cycle. Also, Gantt charts highlight critical dependencies between project tasks, allowing project managers to see which tasks are essential to the project's success and identify potential issues with time and resource management.

To create an effective Gantt chart, understand its key components. These include:

- **Horizontal and Vertical Axis.** The horizontal axis represents the timeline, while the vertical axis shows a project's tasks, activities, or phases.

- **Task Bars.** These are visually represented on the chart by horizontal bars that indicate the start and end dates of each task.

- **Milestones and Markers.** Denote significant events, such as project milestones or the completion of specific tasks.

- **Dependencies and relationships.** Show the relationship between tasks and the order in which they must be completed.

After knowing the components of a Gantt chart, move on to creating one. Here are the steps:

1. **Identify and list all the project tasks.** Make a complete list of all the tasks that need to be performed to complete the project. Break down tasks into smaller, manageable portions.

2. **Assign Resources.** Define the individuals and materials responsible for each task.

3. **Estimate Duration.** For each task, estimate the duration of the task's completion. This assists in determining scheduling, cost, and resource allocations.

4. **Set milestones and deadlines.** Assign standard deadlines and milestones to significant tasks or project phases.

5. **Draw the chart using software or manually.** Choose the tool or software of preference and start creating a chart.

The 4 Pillars of Problem-Solving

However, like any tool, Gantt charts have their limitations. For instance, it assumes that all tasks and activities can be accurately estimated and completed on time. However, unexpected events occur frequently, affecting the overall project timeline. To overcome this limitation, build flexibility and contingency planning into your project plan. For example, add buffer time to your project schedule, or use a PERT chart to estimate project timelines more accurately.

Another limitation of Gantt charts is their limited ability to represent complex relationships between tasks and activities. Gantt charts work well when there is a clear and linear relationship between tasks. Yet, in complex projects with interdependencies and overlapping activities, Gantt charts can become confusing and difficult to manage. To overcome this limitation, use more advanced project management tools, such as critical path analysis or network diagrams. These tools allow you to map out complex relationships and dependencies between tasks and activities more accurately.

Lastly, Gantt charts likely lead to the potential for oversimplification and misinterpretation. As such, it may be attractive and easy to read. Despite that, it can also be oversimplified and lead to misunderstanding the project plan. To overcome this limitation, use Gantt charts with other project management tools, such as work *breakdown structures (WBS) or earned value management (EVM)*. These tools provide a more detailed and accurate view of the project plan, allowing you to make better decisions and avoid misinterpretations.

When selecting a tool for creating and evaluating flowcharts, it is imperative to take your specific needs and budget into consideration. Some tools may be better suited for creating basic diagrams, while others may be more adept at managing complex processes. By utilizing flowcharts, you can identify areas that need improvement and streamline processes to boost the success of your organization.

Chapter 6:
SWOT Analysis

A deep understanding of our strengths, weaknesses, opportunities, and threats is necessary to remain competitive in today's fast-paced environment. Using SWOT analysis, firms and organizations can identify the internal and external factors impacting their performance.

This chapter contains topics tailored to give you an understanding of SWOT analysis. For instance, the step-by-step process of conducting a SWOT analysis is listed below. A section also of this chapter addresses the limitations and essential considerations of SWOT analysis. By understanding the intricacies of SWOT analysis, you can gain valuable insights to help you remain competitive and succeed.

What Is a SWOT Analysis

To help you assess things, SWOT analysis breaks down into four components, such as:

- **Strengths.** Refer to the internal factors that can help your enterprise excel and stay competitive. Strengths can come in many forms, such as skills, unique resources, or advantages over your competitors.

- **Weaknesses.** Resulted from a lack of resources or skills, quality issues, or anything that puts you at a disadvantage against your competitors. Ignoring these internal factors can harm your enterprise and make it less competitive.

- **Opportunities.** Arise from market changes, new technologies, or other factors that you can take advantage of to improve your performance. Hence, these external factors can benefit your enterprise and help you grow.

- **Threats.** Came from many sources, such as competition, market saturation, new regulations, or economic changes. These external factors can harm your enterprise and make it vulnerable to risks.

There are various benefits to using SWOT analysis, including *identifying areas of improvement, capitalizing on opportunities, and making informed decisions.*

Identifying Areas of Improvement

By conducting a SWOT analysis, you can identify the areas of your organization that need improvement. These weaknesses can be analyzed to determine what changes are required to enhance the growth of your organization. For instance, the analysis could reveal a lack of staff, insufficient resources, or the need for training. This information will help identify areas where improvements are needed, leading to improved efficiency, revenue, and customer satisfaction.

Capitalizing on Opportunities

By analyzing the external environment for potential opportunities, businesses can create strategies to tap into new markets, expand their customer base, and increase revenue. Suppose a new technology is emerging that could help you streamline your operations. Early identification of these opportunities can give your organization a competitive advantage.

Making Informed Decisions

Businesses can confidently make decisions by providing a comprehensive overview of their organization's strengths, weaknesses, opportunities, and threats. For example, a SWOT analysis can help determine if it aligns with their overall strategy when considering a new product or service offering. As such, it determines whether you have the resources to execute it effectively or if it addresses a customer need. This information can help businesses avoid costly mistakes in organizational decisions.

The SWOT Analysis Process

Before beginning the SWOT analysis, ensure that you follow the necessary processes.

Identifying the Subject or Problem

To begin the SWOT analysis process, define the specific subject or problem. These subjects could be a product, service, or the entire organization. Likewise, it must be clearly and accurately defined to ensure the analysis remains focused and relevant.

Gathering Internal and External Data

Collect internal and external data to complete a thorough SWOT analysis. Internal data includes information about the subject or problem that is within the control of the business. For instance, it could include financial reports, sales data, employee feedback, and customer satisfaction ratings. External data, on the other hand, provides information about the subject or problem that is outside the business's control. Likely, these data are about industry trends, competitor analysis, and market research.

Identifying Strengths and Weaknesses

Once you have gathered all the necessary data, identify strengths first. These are the areas where the company thrives and has a competitive advantage over competitors. A loyal consumer base, great brand awareness, innovative products, or a trained team are all examples of strengths. Through these strengths, the organization may establish plans that capitalize on these advantages.

Conversely, some weaknesses could hinder your organization's success. Weaknesses refer to areas where the company lacks resources or struggles to compete. Examples of weaknesses include outdated technology, insufficient finances, or low employee morale. Identifying weaknesses can help develop strategies to address and turn them into strengths.

Identifying Opportunities and Threats

Identifying opportunities is the next phase in the SWOT analysis process. These are outside elements that impact the company's growth and profitability. Emerging technologies, new markets, and changes in customer behavior can all create opportunities. Companies can design plans to capitalize on these possibilities and expand their business by identifying them.

Meanwhile, identify potential threats as well. These external elements may harm the company's growth and performance. Increased competition, shifting rules, and economic downturns are examples of dangers. For instance, build plans to prepare for and limit the impact of these dangers by identifying them.

Creating a SWOT Matrix

Construct a SWOT matrix that visually represents the analysis, enabling deep comprehension of the various elements' relationships. The matrix is commonly divided into four quadrants, with the top two featuring strengths and weaknesses and the bottom two containing opportunities and threats. This matrix can be used to create tactics that strengthen current strengths, tackle current weaknesses, capitalize on opportunities, and prepare for potential threats.

Limitations & Considerations

While SWOT analysis provides valuable insights, it also contains limitations, including:

Limited Data and Results

SWOT analysis is sometimes mistaken as a thorough market research technique. In contrast, it is only a simple concept outlining strengths, weaknesses, opportunities, and threats based on existing information and data. Organizations may overlook new opportunities or threats by limiting information to insights from existing data. Hence, consider social, economic, and geographic factors and keep updated information about the market. Analyzing other companies, suppliers, and stakeholders relevant to a particular industry will provide a broader perspective and more accurate results.

Overemphasis and Unreliability

Organizations may overemphasize internal factors such as strengths or overstate external factors they perceive as threats to their business, resulting in an unrealistic or biased interpretation or plan. Inaccurate results could lead to high risks, missed opportunities, or inadequate decision-making. The solution to this issue is to involve participants from different backgrounds, interests, and expertise in conducting a SWOT analysis.

Not Action Oriented

Many executives often use SWOT analysis to lay the groundwork for their strategic planning. However, the value of this process is based on the follow-up and implementation of their result-based strategies and decisions. Strategic planning must be action-oriented and include an action plan for necessary improvements based on the insights and takeaways from the SWOT analysis. Thus, remember that action cultivates growth while a lack of activity stunts it.

To sum it up, stay informed, be flexible, and focus on implementing action plans tailored to your specific business to overcome the limitations of SWOT analysis.

Chapter 7:
Six Sigma Methodology

Every company seeks to deliver quality products and services that meet customer satisfaction and contribute to growth. And to achieve this, companies use different quality assurance and improvement methodologies. One popular methodology that major corporations have widely used is the Six Sigma process.

Six Sigma, a data-driven methodology, uses statistical tools and techniques to lower errors and raise process quality. To gain a profound knowledge of this method, this chapter covers the necessary topics such as six sigma's process, variations, and limitations.

What Is a Six Sigma Methodology

In ensuring quality management, Six Sigma identifies and removes defects in a business process while minimizing variability through its data-driven approach. In fact, this method aims to achieve a level of 3.4 *defects per million opportunities (DPMO),* which translates to a 99.99966% chance of producing a product or delivering a service without defects.

To achieve this goal, the Six Sigma methodology follows a set of concepts and principles, such as customer focus, process orientation, data and fact-based decision-making, leadership, and people involvement. These principles help ensure that the focus remains on fulfilling customer needs and expectations and that business decisions are based on data and facts.

The Six Sigma Process (DMAIC)

Incorporating the Six Sigma methodology can assist you in implementing the five-step process DMAIC: *Define, Measure, Analyze, Improve, and Control*. Each step in DMAIC has its unique goals and objectives, which include:

Define Phase

The goals of the define phase are to define the problem, set clear timelines, and establish goals and objectives that can be quantified and measured. This phase is critical because it sets the foundation for all the other phases in the DMAIC process. During this phase, the project team defines the project's scope, identifies stakeholders, and gathers customer feedback.

Measure Phase

In the measure phase, the team collects data to determine the current state of the process. Likewise, this phase involves analyzing critical process parameters, determining the process capability, and identifying potential sources of variation. Hence, the measure phase aims to establish a baseline for the given process, measuring the effectiveness of changes made during the subsequent phases.

Analyze Phase

During the analysis phase, the team examines the data collected in the measure phase to determine the root cause of the problem. It is critical to identify the root cause to avoid making ineffective changes that do not solve the underlying issue. The root cause analysis helps focus on the main issues, prioritize them, and develop practical and effective solutions.

Improve Phase

Once the project team identifies the problem's root cause, they can move to the improvement phase, where they test the proposed solutions and verify their effectiveness. The team will develop a plan and task list to implement the proposed solution and then make adjustments to optimize the solution. The goal of the improvement phase is to reduce defects and increase efficiency in the process.

Control Phase

This phase is where the project team establishes policies, procedures, and checks that ensure the solution and its effectiveness are sustainable in the long term. During this phase, the project team designs a monitoring mechanism that checks for deviations in the process. Likewise, they develop contingency plans to address deviations from the standard procedure.

Limitations & Considerations

Although organizations have widely adopted the six sigma methodology, some limitations and considerations must be considered. Some of these limitations include:

Complexity

The methodology uses a lot of statistical analysis, which can be challenging and time-consuming for organizations to implement. It also requires specialized knowledge and expertise in statistical analysis, which may not be readily available within an organization. To overcome this limitation, simplify your approach to Six Sigma by focusing on its core principles rather than getting bogged down in the details.

Resistance to Change

Employees may be resistant to new processes or methods, especially if they are unfamiliar with the methodology. Considering that, provide adequate training, communication, and support to help employees adopt and embrace the Six Sigma methodology. By involving employees in the implementation process and explaining the benefits of Six Sigma, businesses can overcome resistance to change and ensure that everyone is on board.

Limited Scope

Six Sigma is designed to achieve a narrow focus on process improvement, which can be both a strength and a limitation. While it can optimize specific processes, it may not be well-suited for broader business strategies. To overcome this limitation, combine Six Sigma with other lean or balanced scorecard methodologies to achieve a more holistic approach to improving their operations.

Overemphasis on Metrics

While data analysis is essential in Six Sigma, it is not the only factor determining success. Metrics should guide problem-solving, but they should not be the only factor driving decisions. To overcome this limitation, focus on setting goals and objectives that align with the overall strategy.

By striking the right balance between statistical analysis and practical knowledge, you can overcome the limitations of Six Sigma and reap its benefits.

Variations

Various variations of the Six Sigma methodology have emerged over the years, and how businesses can use them to optimize their operations. Below are some of the most frequently used versions of Six Sigma:

Design for Six Sigma (DFSS): Designing new goods or procedures is the focus of DFSS, a Six Sigma variant.

The methodology uses a structured approach to design products or processes that meet customer needs and are highly reliable. DFSS incorporates tools and techniques from traditional Six Sigma and other methodologies such as *Design of Experiments (DOE) and Quality Function Deployment (QFD)*.

- **Lean Six Sigma.** A process improvement methodology that focuses on reducing waste and increasing efficiency. For instance, it aims to identify and cut waste through a structured problem-solving approach. It also encompasses six sigma's tools and techniques while incorporating lean principles, such as value stream mapping, Kaizen, and continuous improvement. By combining lean principles with six sigma, companies can achieve significant results in process improvement.

- **Six Sigma for Services.** Tailored to service-based processes. This methodology focuses on improving customer satisfaction, reducing errors, and increasing efficiency in service-based processes. Six Sigma for Services also incorporates tools and techniques from traditional six sigma and other methodologies such as *Customer Relationship Management (CRM) and Voice of the Customer (VOC)*.

- Six Sigma for Software. Variation of Six Sigma for software development processes. As such, it focuses on lowering software development faults and raising software quality. Like the others, it incorporates tools and techniques from traditional Six Sigma and other methodologies such as *Agile Development and Test-Driven Development (TDD)*.

In conclusion, **flow charts and diagrams** are visual tools that provide a clear understanding of a process or system, making it easier to identify areas for improvement. Meanwhile, **SWOT analysis** is a strategic planning technique to identify a company's internal strengths and weaknesses and external opportunities and threats. Conversely, the **Six Sigma methodology** is a data-driven approach focusing on eliminating defects and reducing process variability to improve quality and efficiency. These tools and techniques are essential in problem-solving and process improvement, providing a systematic approach to success in various fields and industries

Pillar 3:
Decide

When it comes to problem-solving, selecting the best course of action from the potential solutions is needed. This pillar, known as the decide phase, requires you to evaluate and prioritize the possible solutions generated in previous stages. In this phase, you will learn how to assess, prioritize, and decide on the most suitable solution that meets the identified problem's needs.

By taking a careful and methodical approach, you can determine the best solution to improve your processes. Remember that careful consideration and attention to detail are essential in this phase, and with the right approach, you can achieve optimal results.

Chapter 8:
Identifying Options

In problem-solving and decision-making, one essential step is identifying viable options. This process entails creating a spectrum of alternatives and assessing the potential benefits and drawbacks. The more alternatives you have, the greater the likelihood of selecting the optimal solution.

Hence, this chapter delves into three techniques that can facilitate the identification of options: *brainstorming sessions, probability analysis, and idea-generation workshops*.

Conduct Brainstorming Sessions

Brainstorming generates fresh ideas and finds innovative solutions in a group setting. These collaborative sessions help businesses, educational institutions, and even creative endeavors to expound ideas. For instance, it encourages out-of-the-box thinking and embracing unconventional ideas. Besides, brainstorming sessions can unlock new realms of creativity and foster active participation from everyone involved.

Behind successful brainstorming sessions lies a healthy environment that encourages participation and collaboration. Hence, choose a peaceful location and establish basic rules that encourage all attendees to contribute equally. For instance, make the guests feel comfortable sharing their ideas without negative criticism. Additionally, participants should be encouraged to build upon each other's suggestions to create more rich and effective solutions.

Likewise, set the right tone and mood before you start the brainstorming process. Once you have created an inviting and inclusive atmosphere, start presenting a specific problem statement or goal for the group to tackle. To ensure everyone is on the same page, participants should be given ample opportunity to ask questions and clarify their understanding of the issue.

Consider utilizing various approaches to maximize creativity and generate a wealth of new ideas during your brainstorming session. For instance, let participants try mind mapping, free writing, or other techniques to explore the problem from different angles and perspectives. To further expand the scope of the discussion, they can also try brainstorming hypothetical scenarios or *"what-if"* scenarios. Mixing up your approach and exploring the issue from multiple angles will make you more likely to uncover innovative and effective solutions.

However, in brainstorming sessions, be aware of their limitations. As such, during brainstorming, there might be a lack of focus or direction, which can arise when participants generate many ideas without a clear plan for assessing or ranking them. Likewise, not all ideas generated during a brainstorming session will be feasible or practical. Establish clear criteria for evaluating and prioritizing the generated ideas to ensure that you make the most of your session. Consequently, these criteria will separate the most promising ideas from those that may not be as viable, ensuring that the resources and efforts are put into the most promising avenues.

Probability Analysis

In numerous fields, probability analysis is a fundamental technique employed to evaluate risks, make informed choices, and plan for what lies ahead. This approach entails allotting probabilities to various possible outcomes or events, relying on past data or specialists' insights.

To conduct probability analysis, identify the risk factors or potential events that could impact your project or organization. Next, gather relevant data and information to help you assess the likelihood of those events. These data may include information on current trends, historical data, professional judgments, and other pertinent data.

After gathering the necessary data, analyze it for patterns or trends to help predict future events. This step requires calculating probabilities and using statistical techniques to determine the likelihood of specific outcomes. For instance, regression analysis can identify trends in historical data and make predictions based on those trends.

Meanwhile, to effectively analyze probabilities, it is imperative to conduct a thorough risk assessment. During a risk assessment, there is a comprehensive evaluation of the potential impact of various risks on your project or organization while determining the likelihood of these risks becoming a reality. By identifying potential hazards and assigning probabilities, you can take proactive measures to mitigate or eliminate these risks. Dividing this process into manageable segments will also help streamline your analysis and optimize your risk management strategy.

In fields where unpredictability and risk are commonplace, such as finance, insurance, or healthcare, probability analysis can be a valuable tool in your arsenal. For instance, in finances, probability analysis can assist in evaluating the possibility of market-related occurrences, such as shifts in interest rates or stock prices. Investors can use this information to make knowledgeable judgments on where to put their money.

Meanwhile, the insurance industry is familiar with how probability analysis can be leveraged to evaluate the probability of particular events, such as natural disasters or accidents. This data is then utilized to determine the premiums that policyholders should pay based on the likelihood of the insured event happening. Probability analysis can also assist insurance companies in identifying potential risks and developing new products to address them, enabling them to provide better coverage to their clients. Understanding how probability analysis works and its benefits helps navigate the complexities of the insurance industry and provides your clients with more effective coverage options.

Conversely, in healthcare, probability analysis helps assess the probability of different diseases and health conditions occurring. Likewise, it predicts the possible outcomes of various treatments. Medical professionals utilize this information to make informed patient care decisions and develop new treatments and medications. Using probability analysis in healthcare means having a deeper appreciation for the complexities of medical decision-making and potentially contributing to advancing the field by developing new and innovative approaches to patient care.

While probability analysis sounds promising, it also has its limitations. For instance, uncovering the accuracy of the utilized assumptions is one of these limits. As such, the estimated probabilities may be incorrect if the analysis's data was biased or was based on a tiny sample size. Hence, to avoid this limitation, ensure that the data used in the analysis is representative and unbiased. Similarly, ensure the sample size is large enough to yield reliable results. Conducting sensitivity analyses and seeking additional data sources can also help mitigate these limitations.

As a highly advanced tool, probability analysis is immensely effective in identifying potential risks, comprehending their impacts, and enabling informed decision-making. This analytical technique is ubiquitous across various sectors, including finance, insurance, healthcare, and beyond. Albeit its limitations, probability analysis helps organizations manage risks and proactively develop plans for the future. For instance, financial institutions use probability analysis to evaluate market risks, health professionals apply it to assess potential treatments and patient outcomes, and insurance companies leverage it to estimate the likelihood of future claims. Despite the complexity involved, learning to apply probability analysis can provide a significant competitive advantage in various industries.

Conduct Idea Generation Workshops

Complex challenges often necessitate ingenious solutions. To overcome these obstacles, recognize and formulate answers to address these problems effectively. One practical way to generate such ideas is by organizing idea-generation workshops. These workshops are excellent for teams to collaborate and brainstorm new concepts that can add value to the organization. To conduct these workshops successfully, here are some tips to keep in mind:

Define the Problem

To start an idea creation workshop, identify the issue or challenge that needs to be solved. This could involve everything from improving a product to boosting sales or cutting expenses. The team may concentrate on finding solutions once the problem has been identified.

Invite the Right Participants

Invite a diverse group of participants to the workshop. People with various backgrounds, experiences, and skill sets must be included. Likewise, invite those willing to give their ideas and have a stake in the issue at hand. Having multiple viewpoints and thoughts in a workshop can lead to a richer and more diverse discussion, fostering learning and generating creative solutions to problems.

Set the Ground Rules

Provide everyone with an equal opportunity to share their ideas. Additionally, the ideas presented should not be judged to maintain a safe and non-judgmental environment. Finally, participants should be encouraged to think outside the box and keep an open mind while brainstorming. By following these ground rules, your workshop can cultivate an atmosphere of collaboration and creativity.

Encourage Idea Generation

Participants should be encouraged to develop as many ideas as possible, build on each other's ideas, and develop new ones. Provide prompts or exercises that stimulate creativity and brainstorming to inspire idea generation. Additionally, it can be helpful to establish a clear goal or problem statement to focus the ideation process and generate more targeted ideas.

Use Visualization Techniques

Visualization techniques can be used to help participants think creatively. For example, ask participants to imagine they are in a different industry and think about how they would solve the problem or challenge. This method can aid in removing mental obstacles and fostering original thought.

Group and Prioritize Ideas

After generating multiple ideas, group them into themes or categories. The key areas of concentration will be easier to determine as a result. Set the ideas in order of importance based on their viability and possible impact. For instance, use a voting or weighted ranking system to do this.

Develop an Action Plan

Once the ideas have been prioritized, develop an action plan. Assign responsibilities and timelines for each idea. Create a plan that is practical, achievable, and measurable. This will ensure that the ideas generated during the workshop are implemented effectively.

Thus, **identifying options** helps in the problem-solving process. Besides that, there are several effective techniques to help generate ideas. For instance, **conducting brainstorming sessions and idea-generation workshops** can lead to diverse and creative ideas from multiple perspectives. Lastly, using **probability analysis** can provide valuable insight into each option's feasibility and potential outcomes

Chapter 9:
Evaluate and Prioritize Solutions

Effective problem-solving requires identifying, creating, and assessing potential solutions. However, it can be challenging without a structured approach to evaluating and prioritizing solutions.

Considering that, this chapter explores techniques that include decision matrices, trees, evaluation criteria, weighting schemes, and scoring. Multi-criteria decision analysis is also discussed for complex alternatives.

Decision Matrices and Decision Trees

A decision matrix is a tool that helps you weigh the pros and cons of different options. Particularly, it is useful when there are multiple criteria to consider. To create a decision matrix, start by identifying your options. Next, list the factors crucial to you, such as price, time, or potential dangers. Then assign a weight to each criterion based on their prominence. For instance, if cost is a significant factor, you can give it more weight than other factors.

Once you have identified the options and criteria, assign a score to each option for each criterion. As such, use a numerical scale, such as 1 to 10, or a descriptive scale, such as *"excellent," "good," "fair," and "poor."* Multiply each score by the weight assigned to the corresponding criterion, and add the results for each option. The choice that most closely matches your criteria is the one with the highest overall score.

Yet, if there are several steps in the decision-making process, a decision tree might help you visualize them. Start with the problem description, then list the possibilities and requirements for each action. For example, deciding on marketing strategy options such as social media, email, or direct mail campaigns can be evaluated based on cost, reach, and effectiveness. Decision trees help organize these complex decisions and make them easier to understand.

Develop Evaluation Criteria

To evaluate potential solutions, establish measurable criteria uniform with the problem statement by doing the following:

1. Review the problem statement carefully to identify the key issues and concerns.

2. Brainstorm a list of potential criteria that can be used to measure the effectiveness of any proposed solutions.

3. Select the most relevant and essential criteria that align with the problem statement and the overall objectives.

4. Ensure the criteria are specific, measurable, achievable, relevant, and time-bound (SMART) to facilitate effective measurement and evaluation.

Evaluation criteria should also be mutually exclusive and collectively exhaustive, meaning they do not overlap and cover all possible solutions. **Mutual exclusivity** implies that each criterion should be independent of the others. Hence, the satisfaction of one criterion should not impact the evaluation of the other criteria. Meanwhile, **collectively exhaustive** entails considering all possible options without any option being overlooked or excluded from consideration. In simpler terms, mutual exclusivity ensures that each criterion is evaluated separately, while collectively exhaustive ensures that no option is left unconsidered.

Additionally, the criteria should be weighted appropriately to reflect their importance to the problem statement. For example, sales increase evaluation criteria may include revenue, profit margin, or customer retention rate. Similarly, to ensure consistency with the problem statement, the evaluation criteria should be directly relevant to the problem you are attempting to solve. Suppose the problem statement revolves around enhancing customer satisfaction. Then, focus on factors influencing consumer happiness, such as response time, product quality, and customer service.

Develop Weighting Schemes

Assigning weights to each evaluation criterion helps prioritize solutions. A weighting scheme should include factors such as cost, time, risk, and impact on employees and customers. Consistency is crucial throughout the problem-solving process to accurately compare different solutions.

Different methods for assigning weights to criteria include *equal weighting, subjective weighting, and analytical weighting.*

- **Equal Weighting.** Allotting equal importance or value to each criterion when evaluating potential solutions. This approach assumes that each criterion is equally vital in determining a solution's effectiveness or feasibility. Using equal weighting ensures that all criteria are considered fairly and that no single criterion dominates the decision-making process.

- **Subjective Weighting.** Giving a numerical value or weight to each criterion based on its relative importance to the problem-solver. For instance, weights are assigned based on personal preference, stakeholder input, or expert opinions. Once the weights are given, the criteria can be evaluated based on their importance.

- **Analytical Weighting.** The process of applying weights to criteria based on how well they relate to the goals of the problem-solving process. It entails using a mathematical model to do this. This approach is useful when the criteria are quantifiable and measurable. Methods like pairwise comparison, the *analytical hierarchy process (AHP)*, and weighted decision matrices are used in analytical weighing.

- **Pairwise Comparison.** A technique for evaluating the relative weight of factors. To give a score based on relative importance, each criterion is compared to every other criterion in a pair. The weights of each criterion are then determined based on the results.

To prioritize potential solutions, develop weighting schemes that assign significance and value to each criterion. There are various methods for assigning weights, including equal, subjective, and analytical methods. Subsequently, ensure consistency to compare solutions accurately.

Evaluate Alternatives Based on Criteria

Once you have established your evaluation criteria and assigned weights to them using a weighting scheme, evaluate the alternatives based on those criteria. In this step, *Multi-Criteria Decision Analysis (MCDA) framework* is used to assess complex alternatives using various criteria. As such, MCDA helps problem-solvers to make objective decisions by providing a structured approach to evaluating alternatives.

Multi-criteria Decision Analysis (MCDA) for Complex Alternatives

Multi-Criteria Decision Analysis (MCDA) framework entails segmenting a problem into smaller components and giving weights to each component. After evaluating possibilities using these weights, the optimal option is chosen. To assist problem-solvers in evaluating alternatives, MCDA employs both qualitative and quantitative methods.

Commonly, MCDA is used when making solutions to complex issues, such as environmental or public policy issues. Likewise, it is helpful in the private sector for strategic problem-solving and project management. MCDA also offers a framework for assigning weights to different criteria to prioritize certain criteria over others based on their significance. For instance, when assessing solutions for an environmental issue, MCDA allows setting more weight to criteria like sustainability and environmental impact while assigning less weight to criteria such as cost and time.

There are various tools in MCDA to evaluate options, such as decision matrices, decision trees, and utility analysis. Decision matrices are commonly used in MCDA to evaluate options based on multiple criteria. As such, it involves listing the criteria on the top and the options on the side. Each cell in the matrix is filled with scores representing how well each option performs on each criterion. The scores are then weighted according to the importance of each criterion; the option with the highest weighted score is considered the best solution.

Meanwhile, decision trees evaluate alternatives. These trees consist of a series of decision points and possible outcomes of a decision. For instance, it allows comprehending each choice's results and making well-informed decisions. By using decision trees, problem-solvers can better understand the potential consequences of each option and weigh their choices accordingly.

Utility analysis is one of the many techniques employed in MCDA. In this method, numerical values are assigned to each criterion and alternative based on their perceived value, which is then weighted to reflect their relative importance. Subsequently, the alternative with the highest overall value is considered the most optimal solution. Adopting this approach ensures accurate evaluation of each option's value and determines the best action.

While MCDA offers several benefits, it can be time-consuming and resource-intensive, primarily when evaluating complex alternatives with many criteria. Additionally, MCDA's effectiveness depends on the accuracy of the data and assumptions used to evaluate alternatives, which can be challenging to estimate with certainty.

Despite that, there are several ways to overcome the challenges associated with using MCDA for evaluating complex alternatives:

- **Utilize expert judgment.** Experts in the relevant fields can provide valuable insight into data accuracy and assumptions used to evaluate alternatives. Their input can help refine and improve the decision-making process.

- **Conduct sensitivity analyses.** By varying the input data and assumptions used in the MCDA, sensitivity analyses can help assess the robustness of the results and identify the most critical factors driving the decision.

- **Use software tools.** Various software tools are available to assist with the MCDA process, which can streamline and automate the process, reducing the time and resources required.

Evaluating and prioritizing potential solutions requires decision matrices, trees, and evaluation criteria. Then, **weighting schemes** help to give importance to the criteria based on their relevance. Moreover, multi-criteria decision analysis **(MCDA)** is a helpful technique for evaluating complex alternatives that involve multiple criteria. By utilizing these tools, one can make informed decisions and select the most optimal solution to the problem at hand.

Chapter 10:
Making Decisions

Making decisions involves assessing and mitigating risks, analyzing uncertainties, and selecting the best solution. Under this chapter are various methods and techniques for evaluating risk and uncertainty, refining and selecting the best solution, and checking the Pareto principle.

Assessing Risk and Uncertainty

In the decision-making process, assessing risk and uncertainty is crucial. To make informed decisions, understand the potential outcomes, including the costs and benefits of each option. This requires examining all variables and circumstances that may influence the outcome. Subsequently, it will help explain the risks and uncertainties associated with each option.

There are two effective ways to assess risk: *identifying potential risks and devising strategies to handle them.*

Risk Assessment & Mitigation Plans

Decision-makers can reduce the probability and impact of poor outcomes by identifying potential risks and implementing effective mitigation procedures.

In risk assessment, the first step is to **identify potential hazards**. As such, be thorough in the identification process by considering internal and external factors that may affect the outcome. There are various ways to do this, such as *brainstorming, analyzing past experiences, and seeking expert advice*. After identifying potential dangers, **evaluate the probability and impact** of each risk. This step involves analyzing factors such as the possibility of the risk occurring, the severity of its consequences, and the timing of its occurrence. By prioritizing risks based on these criteria, you can focus on developing mitigation strategies for the most significant risks.

Subsequently, **mitigation plans** must be developed to minimize the impact of the identified risks. Several mitigation measures can be taken, such as avoiding the risk altogether, transferring the risk to another party, reducing the probability of the risk occurring, or limiting the severity of the risk if it does happen.

For creating mitigation strategies, utilize a risk matrix to plot risks on a matrix based on their likelihood and impact. Risks with a high probability of occurrence and significant effects are prioritized for mitigation planning. Conversely, risks that are less likely to occur and have a relatively small impact are given lower priority.

Alternatively, a risk register is an effective tool for mitigation planning. This document describes each identified risk, its probability, impact, and the mitigation techniques that will be implemented to address it.

The risk register can also track progress in adopting mitigation methods and ongoing efficacy.

Thus, risk assessment and mitigation tactics should be integrated as continual procedures. New hazards should be added to the risk register as they emerge, and mitigation measures should be updated accordingly. Regularly assessing and mitigating risks can help make informed decisions and minimize the potential and impact of unfavorable outcomes.

Scenario Analysis

Creating multiple scenarios that represent various outcomes aids in evaluating the impact of each risk. To conduct a scenario analysis, **identify the key drivers** that could impact the outcome of your decision. For instance, it could be factors such as shifting consumer preferences, altered market conditions, or changes in legal requirements. Once these key drivers have been identified**, create scenarios** that represent different outcomes based on changes in these drivers.

Imagine a hypothetical situation where a business is contemplating launching a new product. To assess the potential success of the product launch, the decision-makers must first identify the key drivers that could influence its outcome. These drivers might include customer preferences, pricing strategies, and competition changes. Once these drivers have been identified, the decision-makers can create a variety of scenarios that represent different potential outcomes. These scenarios could include *a best-case scenario, a worst-case scenario, and a most likely scenario based on the identified factors.*

In the **best-case scenario**, the product is in high demand, priced competitively, and has minimal market competition. Conversely, in the

worst-case scenario, the product is overpriced, demand is low, and intense market competition exists. For the **most likely scenario**, the company expects the product to have moderate demand, be competitively priced, and face some market competition.

After creating the scenarios, decision-makers can **evaluate each scenario's potential impact** on the decision. They can assess the financial implications, such as potential revenue and profit margins. Similarly, it can be easier to identify operational implications, such as changes to production processes and staffing requirements.

By assessing these scenarios, decision-makers can identify potential obstacles and develop contingency plans to mitigate risks. Thus, reducing the likelihood of unexpected issues increases the decision's success.

However, there are also some disadvantages to scenario analysis that decision-makers should be aware of. For instance, it relies on assumptions about the key drivers that may affect the decision, which could be incorrect. Also, developing multiple scenarios and assessing the potential impact of each one can be time-consuming. Despite these limitations, sensitivity analysis can help decision-makers overcome these constraints. The sensitivity analysis technique examines the resilience of choice by altering the assumptions utilized in the study. As such, this process explores how the analysis's results would vary if critical assumptions were modified.

Sensitivity Analysis

Sensitivity analysis allows you to evaluate how sensitive a decision or strategy is to changes in key factors. By applying sensitivity analysis, you can understand how changes in assumptions affect the outcome, which is essential in testing the robustness of your decision or strategy.

Aside from that, sensitivity analysis aims to pinpoint the essential assumptions that form the basis of a decision or strategy. Likewise, it assesses how alterations in these assumptions could impact the result. This kind of analysis is valuable because it helps problem-solvers to appraise the hazards and uncertainties linked with a decision and develop backup plans if things go awry.

Moreover, sensitivity analysis entails modifying one or more assumptions and analyzing the consequences. A firm, for example, may seek to assess the impact of changing market circumstances on its revenue estimates. The corporation might experiment with pricing, volume, and market share assumptions to see how these affect revenue.

Various techniques are used in sensitivity analysis, including *one-way analysis, multi-way analysis, and tornado diagrams.* The **one-way analysis** involves changing one assumption at a time while keeping the others constant. This technique helps identify the most crucial assumptions and understand how changes in these assumptions could affect the outcome. Then, **multi-way analysis** involves changing multiple assumptions simultaneously to see how they interact. Hence, it shows how different assumptions might interact and affect the outcome.

Meanwhile, **tornado diagrams** are a graphical representation of sensitivity analysis demonstrating how changes in different assumptions affect the outcome. The assumptions are listed on the horizontal axis, and the impact on the outcome is shown on the vertical axis. As such, the height of the bars indicates how sensitive the result is to variations in each assumption.

Subsequently, sensitivity analysis can be used to assess the effect of interest rate changes on investment decisions or the impact of production cost changes on profitability. Lastly, it evaluates risks and uncertainties associated with different scenarios to identify potential problems in advance and create solutions for them.

Refine and Select the Best Solution

In making decisions, refine the evaluation and prioritization stage results to select the best solution. This process involves considering each solution's feasibility, cost, and potential risks and benefits. It may also include consulting with stakeholders and considering their perspectives.

Once the best solution has been chosen, develop an action plan that outlines the necessary steps to implement it efficiently. The action plan should establish clear deadlines, roles, and materials to achieve the desired outcome. Regular progress updates and evaluations should also be scheduled to verify that the solution functions as expected.

Check the Pareto Principle

When faced with multiple options, the Pareto principle, also known as the 80/20 rule, can assist you in selecting the best option. This rule suggests that only around 20% of the causes lead to 80% of the effects. By identifying the root causes of a problem using this principle, you can focus your efforts on the most critical areas for improvement, resulting in more effective problem-solving.

To apply the Pareto Principle to solution selection, determine the most critical factors contributing to the problem. Then, evaluate potential solutions based on how much impact they would have on these critical factors. This helps to prioritize solutions that are most likely to have the biggest impact on solving the problem.

The 4 Pillars of Problem-Solving

Imagine that a business is experiencing a decline in sales. Upon analyzing the situation, they devise a list of possible solutions, such as reducing prices, boosting advertising, and enhancing product quality. Applying the Pareto principle entails identifying the primary causes of the sales decrease, such as subpar product quality and inadequate brand recognition. Afterward, the business assesses each solution's impact on these factors.

To refine and select the best solution, analyze and compare different options using a formal decision-making process, like a decision matrix or decision tree. The **decision matrix** involves listing all the alternative solutions and evaluating them against criteria. Meanwhile, a **decision tree** uses a graphical representation to map out all possible outcomes and probabilities. Both approaches help to make the decision-making process more structured and objective.

Likewise, consider aspects like *viability, efficacy, cost, and impact* while evaluating solutions. How simple it is to put a solution into action is referred to as **feasibility**. **Effectiveness** is the measure of how well a solution solves a given issue. Then, the **cost** is the monetary expense of implementing the solution. Meanwhile, the **impact** is used to describe the potential effects that a solution might have on an issue.

Overall, when selecting a solution, ensure that all viewpoints are considered and that everyone agrees with the final decision.

Chapter 11:
Implementing the Solution

Once identifying a problem and generating possible solutions are done, the next step is implementing the solution. That said, this chapter focuses on the various aspects of implementing a solution to help you throughout the process. For instance, these practices include creating an action plan, assigning responsibilities and resources, developing a timeline and milestones, monitoring progress, and making adjustments.

Creating an Action Plan

In any field you find, having an action plan is vital as it sets the tone for success. An action plan is a roadmap for achieving a set of objectives that are designed to meet specific goals. It outlines your strategies, the necessary resources, responsibilities, and timelines for your work. And a well-designed action plan ensures that the desired outcome is clear and achievable.

To create an effective action plan, **establish priorities and timelines**. Prioritizing means identifying the actions that will yield the most significant results within a given time frame. As such, you can create priorities using the Pareto principle, which states the 80/20 rule. After identifying your priorities, **develop a timeline** for each task. A timeline ensures that your team knows the deadlines and the importance of sticking to them and can make the necessary adjustments.

Identifying necessary resources is also a significant step in creating an action plan. Necessary resources include funds, workforce, equipment, and technology. Ensure that each help is available where and when it is needed. **Assigning responsibilities** is also essential. For instance, designate specific roles and responsibilities to your team members, aligning them with your priorities and timelines. This way, everyone knows what is expected of them and has a sense of ownership of a task.

Meanwhile, **developing a communication plan** helps you and your team stay updated on your progress. Additionally, communication is crucial when managing stakeholders and customers; it helps them understand your actions and what to expect in the future. When creating a communication plan, *identify the audience, the delivery channel, the message, and the frequency of communication.*

Moreover, identifying potential obstacles and **developing contingency plans** is vital when developing an action plan. Unexpected situations may arise, so it is necessary to identify potential obstacles to achieving your goals. Additionally, contingency plans enable you to plan how to respond to issues whenever they arise, decreasing the risks of failure.

Lastly, **evaluation** is just as necessary as developing an action plan. Measuring success against objectives provides feedback on the effectiveness of your action plan. If the results from your plan show that you have not met the expected objectives, the evaluation helps identify the weak spots and enables you to adjust your strategy. Identifying the strengths and weaknesses of the plan allows you to focus on methods that work. Also, evaluating a plan helps you identify areas for improvement, ensuring that you learn from past mistakes.

Developing a Timeline and Milestones

Developing a timeline and milestones ensures the successful implementation of solutions to problems as it helps track progress, measure performance, and stay on schedule. In grasping this process, we will use a situational example to illustrate how to create a timeline and milestones to address a problem.

When making a timeline, **identify the problem and potential solutions first**. *Suppose the problem is a high employee turnover rate in a company. The possible solutions include improving employee benefits, increasing salaries, and providing more training opportunities.*

Once the potential solutions have been identified, **prioritize them based on their potential impact and feasibility**. *In our example, the company may prioritize improving employee benefits since it is more feasible. Likewise, it can impact employee retention more than increasing salaries or providing more training opportunities.*

To develop a timeline, **specify the steps for each solution and estimate the time needed for each step**. *In our example, the necessary steps for improving employee benefits include conducting employee surveys, researching industry standards, and negotiating with insurance providers. The estimation for each step is two to four weeks, depending on the complexity and availability of resources.*

In addition to developing a timeline, **establish milestones** to measure progress and celebrate achievements. To be useful, milestones must be specific, measurable, achievable, relevant, and time-bound (SMART). *In our example, significant events or checkpoints may include completing employee surveys, finalizing the new benefits package, and communicating the changes to employees. Approximately each milestone may take four to six weeks to complete.*

Moreover, the *critical path diagram and the Gantt chart could help* make the timeline. A **Gantt chart** is a visual representation that displays each task's start and end times, duration, and dependencies. For instance, it is beneficial for managing and overseeing a project. In contrast, the **critical path diagram** shows the sequence of tasks that must be completed before the project can be considered a success.

By identifying the necessary steps, estimating the time needed, and establishing significant events or checkpoints, we can track progress, measure performance, and ensure that each step is completed on time.

Monitoring Progress

Monitoring progress ensures that solutions to a problem are working effectively and efficiently. For instance, it helps identify any deviations from the plan and allows timely corrections. To further illustrate this process, let us use a situational example showing all the necessary steps you need to follow.

Suppose an organization is facing the problem of high employee turnover rates. To address this problem, they have implemented several solutions, including improving employee benefits, offering more training opportunities, and enhancing the company culture. The organization needs to monitor the progress of these solutions to ensure that they effectively reduce employee turnover rates.

First, the organization **established performance metrics**. Under this step is the **identification of key performance (KPI)**. Subsequently, they identified KPIs such as employee satisfaction, retention rates, and feedback. After that, the organization needs to **set target values for KPIs**. As such, they set target values for these KPIs, intending to achieve a 20% increase in employee satisfaction, a 15% reduction in employee turnover rates, and a 50% increase in employee feedback.

After that, **collecting data** is necessary. For instance, the organization has **developed a plan to collect data** regularly to monitor progress toward the set KPIs. Then, they **identified the data sources**, including employee feedback surveys, exit interviews, and performance evaluations. Likewise, they plan to **gather data at regular intervals**, such as quarterly or semi-annually.

Subsequently, the organization **reviews the collected data to identify trends and patterns** indicating progress or areas requiring improvement. With the collected information, they **compare the collected data to the target values** established for each KPI to determine if progress is being made. The company also **identifies areas of improvement** that can be made based on the analysis of the collected data.

Based on the evaluation results, the organization **makes necessary changes** to improve the effectiveness of the implemented solutions. They also **continuously monitor progress** toward achieving the established KPIs. Other than that, based on the evaluation results, the organization **refines KPIs and performance metrics as needed.**

Making Adjustments

Implementing a solution is the first step toward achieving the desired outcome in any problem-solving process. However, sometimes the implemented solution may fail to deliver the expected results due to unforeseen circumstances or factors. In such cases, adjusting the solution ensures the objective is still met.

In making adjustments to a failed solution, **identify first that it has failed**. Some signs of the solution failing may include not meeting performance targets, customer complaints, or decreased productivity. Gathering data to confirm the failure is also essential to ensure that it does not result from a temporary issue that will resolve itself.

After identifying the failure, the next step is to **analyze it**. Possible reasons for the failure include inadequate resources, poor implementation, or a lack of clear objectives. Identifying the root cause of the failure is essential to develop effective solutions that address the underlying issue. Likewise, learn from the failure to avoid similar mistakes in the future.

Once the failure has been analyzed, **brainstorm new solutions**. Encouraging creative thinking and considering alternative approaches can lead to more effective solutions that address the root cause of the failure. Developing new solutions may involve redefining objectives, adjusting processes, or seeking input from different stakeholders.

Moreover, developing a plan for implementing the new solution ensures it is implemented effectively. Communicating the plan to all stakeholders is also essential to ensure everyone is on the same page. When obtaining the necessary resources to implement the new solution, seek additional funding, train staff, or acquire new equipment.

After that, **establishing metrics** for evaluating the success of the new solution ensures that it is working as intended. Monitoring progress towards the objectives and making adjustments as needed until it delivers the desired results.

To maintain effectiveness during implementation, adaptability and open-mindedness are essential. Although a clear plan and objectives are important, it is necessary to remain flexible in the face of changing circumstances. This could include revising timelines or priorities based on feedback from team members and stakeholders. Staying open to adjustments makes it possible to keep the project on track and achieve the desired results.

Pillar 4:
Overcome

In this final pillar, learn how to overcome the limitations and challenges that may arise as you apply this problem-solving process. These challenges may include a lack of clarity, biases, assumptions, time constraints, and resource limitations.

Chapter 12:
Lack of Clarity

As such, working on a problem is likely frustrating and challenging when faced with unclear objectives or undefined steps. In fact, ambiguity, confusion, and poor decision-making often stem from a lack of clarity. Hence, to ensure effective problem-solving, clarity is of utmost importance.

For instance, this chapter delves into the sources of confusion and ambiguity while exploring methods for breaking down problems into smaller components. Likewise, it contains ways to refine problem statements and objectives through iterative feedback and testing.

Identifying Sources of Confusion

Identifying sources of confusion or ambiguity is crucial in solving any problem. Knowing precisely what you want to happen is the first step toward problem-solving. However, without clarity, the problem solver risks solving the wrong problem. This lack of clarity often stems from a poorly defined problem statement or unclear objectives.

Considering that, it is necessary to deconstruct the ambiguity problem into its parts before trying to solve it. For example, computer science and mathematics employ this strategy, *"divide and conquer."* Breaking down the problem into smaller, more manageable components makes it easier to identify the sources of confusion or ambiguity.

The *"divide and conquer"* strategy is a problem-solving technique that involves breaking a complex problem into smaller subproblems and addressing them individually. This approach can be applied to various issues, such as developing software or formulating a company strategy. To effectively use this strategy, break down the problem into the smallest possible subproblems and solve each subproblem independently.

Moreover, the *"divide and conquer"* strategy has a lot of advantages. First, it allows disassembling of a problem into smaller parts and aids in reducing its complexity. This can simplify comprehending and pinpointing the causes of ambiguity or confusion. Second, it allows for more efficient problem-solving by solving each sub-problem independently. Finally, it can help to identify potential solutions that may not have been apparent when looking at the problem as a whole.

Refining the problem definition and objectives through iterative feedback and testing is an essential strategy to address confusion and ambiguity. This process involves continually evaluating and refining the problem statement and objectives until they are clear and well-defined. Through iterative feedback and testing, individuals and teams can ensure that the problem statement and objectives are well-defined and aligned with the desired outcome.

Iterative feedback and testing comprise a set of actions that can help refine problem statements and objectives. To begin, the problem statement and objectives should be articulated as clearly and concisely as possible. Subsequently, potential solutions are generated and tested to see if they effectively address the problem and accomplish the objectives. Based on the results of these tests, the problem statement and objectives are modified, and the process is repeated until an optimal solution is attained.

The iterative feedback and testing approach has many benefits. First, it ensures that the problem statement and objectives are well-defined and aligned with the desired outcome. Second, it assists in locating potential answers that might not have been obvious initially. Finally, it allows for continuous improvement by refining the problem statement and objectives based on feedback from testing.

Hence, when tackling a problem, pinpoint first the factors causing confusion or ambiguity. The desired outcome should also be explicitly stated to ensure success, and the problem statement and objectives should be well-defined and aligned with the intended outcome. One strategy for breaking down a problem into more manageable parts is the *"divide and conquer"* approach, which can help reveal areas of uncertainty or confusion.

By utilizing iterative feedback and testing, you can continuously improve and perfect your problem statement and objectives until a satisfactory solution is achieved. This approach allows you to effectively and efficiently address sources of confusion or uncertainty, resulting in more successful outcomes for your problem-solving endeavors.

Breaking Down the Problem

Breaking down a large project into smaller, more manageable tasks can benefit project managers by enabling them to assign tasks to team members and monitor progress more effectively. Smaller projects are also easier to manage in terms of risk identification, resource allocation, and progress tracking.

Moreover, breaking complex problems into smaller components can facilitate problem-solving by making it less daunting and more adaptable to changes. Tackling a problem as a single, monolithic task can be overwhelming, making it challenging to pivot and adjust course when unexpected obstacles arise. Smaller tasks offer the flexibility and adaptability to navigate unexpected changes and achieve more successful outcomes.

Collaboration and teamwork can be improved when a problem is divided into smaller components. For instance, team members can take ownership of different parts of the problem, bringing their expertise and perspectives. This approach can lead to more original solutions and better-shared accountability.

There are various methods to break a problem into smaller parts. One common method is creating a mental map, also known as a mind map. This map type visualizes a problem, with the central idea placed in the center and sub-ideas branching out in various directions. Besides that, it is useful in exploring different ideas and perspectives and identifying key relationships and connections among other problem components.

Aside from mind maps and task breakdown structures, there are various other approaches for breaking down a problem into smaller components: *root cause analysis, Pareto analysis, and fishbone diagrams.* Each of these strategies has advantages and disadvantages, and the technique used will be determined by the problem's nature and the problem solver's specific demands.

Thus, breaking an issue into smaller components is important in problem resolution. This strategy promotes increased comprehension, flexibility, teamwork, and adaptation. When a problem is split into smaller parts, managing, monitoring development, and assigning resources is simpler.

Refining the Problem Statement and Objectives

The problem statement is the foundation of the entire problem-solving process. A well-crafted problem statement provides the problem-solving effort clarity, direction, and purpose. Refining the problem statement involves identifying the problem, describing its severity, and outlining its impact. Techniques for determining the problem statement include brainstorming, creating a problem statement frame, root cause analysis, and SWOT analysis.

Meanwhile, clarifying the problem involves defining it and determining its scope. Likewise, it ensures that all stakeholders understand the problem and that everyone is on the same page. Asking open-ended questions, brainstorming, conducting research, and identifying assumptions and biases can help clarify the problem.

After refining the problem statement, the next step is to redevelop measurable and achievable objectives. Objectives serve as a roadmap for solving the problem, providing specific and realistic targets to strive for. Using the SMART criteria for developing objectives ensures they are specific, measurable, achievable, relevant, and time-bound.

Moreover, developing objectives include identifying the solution domain, prioritizing goals, breaking down objectives into sub-tasks, defining metrics and indicators, and setting deadlines and milestones. Linking objectives to the problem statement ensures that objectives are aligned with the problem statement and contribute to the solution.

Problem framing and reframing can enhance creativity and innovation, collaboration and teamwork, and efficiency and productivity. Techniques for problem framing and reframing include boundary examination, challenging assumptions, divergent thinking, and analogies.

Boundary examination involves identifying the boundaries of the problem and thinking outside the box to explore solutions. Challenging assumptions involves questioning assumptions to identify hidden biases and find new solutions. Then, divergent thinking involves generating multiple solutions to a problem. Meanwhile, analogies involve comparing the problem to other situations and finding similarities to create solutions.

In conclusion, refining the problem statement and objectives is essential for effective problem-solving. A clear problem statement and well-defined objectives guide the problem-solving process, leading to efficient and effective solutions. Techniques include defining the problem statement and using SMART criteria for developing objectives. Lastly, problem framing and reframing can help refine the problem statement and objectives and improve problem-solving.

Chapter 13:
Biases & Assumptions

Regarding problem-solving and decision-making, biases and assumptions can impede progress and negatively impact the outcome. These biases and presumptions can skew reality, hinder creative thinking, and reduce the likelihood of innovation. Consequently, it is crucial to be aware of these biases and assumptions and take measures to counteract them. This chapter will explore a range of strategies aimed at identifying, clarifying, questioning, and challenging biases and assumptions. Additionally, this chapter will also discuss techniques for collecting diverse perspectives and feedback, as well as methods for testing assumptions and biases through experimentation and data analysis.

Identifying Potential Sources of Bias and Assumptions

Identifying potential sources of bias and assumptions is critical in problem-solving and decision-making processes. Biases can affect our judgment, leading to irrational, inaccurate, or unfair decisions. Then, assumptions can mislead us into incorrect judgments about the problem, causing us to overlook crucial information or solutions.

One common source of bias is **personal beliefs and values**. These opinions and principles can impact our decision-making and perception of the world. For instance, if someone strongly believes in a specific political ideology, they may dismiss evidence that contradicts their beliefs. Likewise, if someone emotionally attaches to a particular solution, they may overlook its flaws.

Sometimes, biases and assumptions arise from a lack of information or understanding. As such, limited data makes us use our presumptions to satisfy our curious minds. Suppose you are unfamiliar with a particular culture or population. Then, there is no available information that can fill you up. In such instances, our brains generate generalizations or prejudices to conclude. However, this approach may lead to incorrect assumptions and potentially biased judgments.

Cultural norms and stereotypes can also cause biases and presumptions. Our views, values, and perceptions of other people can all be influenced by our cultural heritage. Stereotypes can lead to incorrect assumptions about individuals or groups and perpetuate biases and discrimination.

Another potential cause of prejudice and presumptions is **groupthink**. Groupthink emerges when a group favors consensus and uniformity above independent thought and analysis. In a groupthink situation, individuals may suppress their doubts or dissenting opinions to maintain group harmony. This can lead to biases and assumptions that go unchallenged, resulting in flawed decision-making.

There are two essential actions to identify potential sources of bias and assumptions: *engage in self-reflection and seek feedback from others*. **Self-reflection** involves examining our own beliefs and values, as well as our decision-making processes. Through this process, we can identify potential biases and assumptions affecting our judgment.

Seeking feedback from others also helps us identify biases and assumptions we may not be aware of. This can involve asking colleagues or stakeholders for input or using tools such as surveys or focus groups to gather diverse perspectives. Likewise, it can help uncover potential prejudices or presumptions we may not be aware of. For instance, soliciting diverse perspectives and input can provide a complete understanding of the problem and potential solutions. By doing so, we can confront our biases and improve the quality of our decisions.

Clarifying Assumptions and Defining Key Terms

Defining key terms and clarifying assumptions are crucial steps in problem-solving and decision-making. This is because stakeholders often have different interpretations of the problem, its causes, and its potential solutions. These differences can arise from individual beliefs, values, cultural norms, and professional expertise. By clarifying assumptions and defining key terms, stakeholders can ensure they share a common understanding of the problem and its potential solutions. Besides that, it helps avoid misunderstandings and allows stakeholders to work more effectively toward a resolution.

One way to clarify assumptions and define key terms is through research. **Research** can help stakeholders comprehensively understand the problem, its causes, impacts, and potential solutions. This method can uncover any knowledge or comprehension gaps contributing to the issue. Research can be conducted using various means, such as literature reviews, surveys, interviews, and case studies. By gathering information from multiple sources, stakeholders can better understand the problem and develop a more informed approach to problem-solving and decision-making.

Consulting with experts is another method to clarify assumptions and define key terms. Experts can provide valuable insights and perspectives, including potential solutions. They can also help identify any biases or assumptions influencing stakeholders' thinking. Meetings, workshops, and online forums are all ways to engage with experts. By consulting with experts, stakeholders can gain a deeper understanding of the problem and develop a more effective strategy for problem-solving and decision-making.

Engaging in open dialogue with stakeholders also helps clarify assumptions and define key terms. This involves creating an open, collaborative environment where stakeholders can share their perspectives and insights. During open discussions, being receptive to all viewpoints and considering various ideas is essential. This can help to identify potential biases or assumptions and develop a shared understanding of the problem and its solutions.

Thus, being clear and precise in the language is critical when defining key terms and clarifying assumptions. Key terms and assumptions should also be clearly defined and transparently identified. Moreover, it ensures that all stakeholders share a common understanding of the problem and its potential solutions.

Suppose a team is working to enhance customer satisfaction in a call center. In this scenario, assumptions include the belief that customers are unhappy with the call center because of long wait times or unresponsive representatives. However, these assumptions may not be correct, and the team may need to research or interact with customers to understand the problem better. In this case, key terms might include *"customer satisfaction,"* which could be defined as specific metrics or indicators, such as wait times or response rates.

Questioning Assumptions and Challenging Biases

Questioning assumptions and challenging biases is vital in problem-solving and decision-making processes. It ensures that decisions are based on sound evidence and logical reasoning rather than personal biases or beliefs. Biases and assumptions can be challenging to detect and often go unchallenged unless individuals actively search for them.

An effective way to challenge biases and assumptions is to **seek information contradicting one's preexisting beliefs.** This involves being open to different perspectives and actively engaging with ideas that may challenge one's assumptions. Also, approach these ideas with an open and curious mindset, rather than a defensive or closed mindset, to fully understand their potential value.

A different approach to addressing biases and presumptions is **engaging with diverse viewpoints or experiences**, which can help identify potential biases and presumptions. Engaging in open and honest dialogue with stakeholders is another effective approach to addressing biases and assumptions. This can involve seeking feedback from people with diverse viewpoints or experiences and carefully listening to their ideas and concerns. To encourage open communication, creating a comfortable and non-judgmental setting for these dialogues is critical.

Aside from that, individuals must be willing to acknowledge their mistakes and be vulnerable to challenge preconceptions and biases. For instance, it is crucial to approach these discussions with humility and an openness to learning rather than defensiveness. Doing so fosters a culture of trust and collaboration where stakeholders feel safe to challenge assumptions and biases without fear of negative consequences.

Likewise, to challenge biases and assumptions, question the language used to describe a problem. Clear and precise definitions of key terms and concepts are also necessary to ensure that all stakeholders have a shared understanding of the problem and potential solutions.

Gathering Diverse Input

Gathering diverse perspectives and input is essential to effective problem-solving and decision-making. By seeking out a wide range of viewpoints and opinions, it is possible to develop a comprehensive understanding of the problem and its potential solutions. Also, it can mitigate the impact of biases and assumptions and uncover new and innovative ideas.

Furthermore, diverse perspectives and input are often gained through surveys or focus groups. These tools are useful for eliciting customer, employee, or community feedback. For instance, **surveys** can be conducted in different formats, such as online or paper-based, and can gather quantitative or qualitative data.

In contrast, **focus groups** typically involve fewer stakeholders who are brought together to discuss a specific topic or issue. These sessions are usually moderated by a facilitator who guides the discussion and ensures all participants can express their opinions and ideas.

Open dialogue with stakeholders is also crucial. This method may involve holding town hall meetings or public forums where stakeholders can discuss issues and provide their viewpoints. Additionally,

one-on-one meetings with stakeholders can provide a more in-depth understanding of their concerns and desires.

To gather diverse perspectives and input effectively, one must be **open to different viewpoints and consider all feedback without prejudice or bias.** This requires active listening and being receptive to constructive criticism. Additionally, it calls for an open and non-judgmental attitude toward different perspectives and viewpoints.

Establishing clear ground rules for discussions can ensure that all stakeholders have an equal opportunity to share their perspectives. Guidelines for respectful and constructive dialogue and rules for ensuring that all voices are heard and no one dominates the conversation can be established to achieve this.

In addition to gathering diverse viewpoints and feedback, it is essential to **ensure that all stakeholders have an opportunity to participate in problem-solving and decision-making.** This can be achieved by creating committees or working groups that include members from diverse stakeholder groups. It may also involve offering training and assistance to stakeholders who lack the necessary skills or experience to engage in the process effectively.

Gathering diverse perspectives and input and ensuring stakeholder participation in decision-making can foster trust and collaboration. This can create a sense of investment in the process and identify solutions that all stakeholders are more likely to accept and implement. Then, **building trust and collaboration** promotes a sense of ownership and encourages all stakeholders to work together towards a common goal.

Testing Assumptions and Biases

Another example of challenging assumptions and biases is product design. Designers often make assumptions about what features or designs will appeal to their target audience, but these assumptions may be based on personal biases or limited data. User testing and data analysis can help designers test their assumptions and gain insights into the needs and preferences of their target audience.

Testing assumptions and biases through experimentation and data analysis requires a rigorous and systematic approach. First, clear hypotheses must be developed, and experiments carefully designed to test them. Next, data must be collected and analyzed objectively and unbiasedly. Finally, conclusions should be drawn based on the evidence rather than preconceived notions. This approach is crucial to ensure that the testing process effectively identifies and challenges assumptions and biases.

Feedback and evaluation should also be incorporated into problem-solving and decision-making processes when evaluating assumptions and biases through experimentation and data analysis. This can help identify areas for improvement and ensure that solutions are effective and sustainable. Then, different approaches, such as surveys, performance indicators, and consumer feedback, can be used to collect feedback and evaluate progress. Conversely, actively seeking feedback and being open to criticism is essential to uncovering blind spots and areas for growth.

In conclusion, biases and assumptions can significantly impact problem-solving and decision-making processes. They can distort reality and limit creative thinking, reducing innovation potential. Therefore, it is essential to be aware of these biases and assumptions and take steps to counteract them.

Chapter 14:
Time & Resource Constraints

Time and resource constraints are a common challenge for individuals and organizations. It can impact productivity, innovation, and success. Due to that, this chapter will explore strategies to prioritize tasks and goals, streamline processes, and use resources effectively. Aside from that, discover creative problem-solving and innovation.

Prioritizing Tasks and Goals

Effective time management and prioritization skills are crucial for personal and professional success. Prioritizing involves identifying the most important tasks and goals and completing them first to maximize productivity and efficiency. However, it can be challenging when facing numerous tasks and approaching deadlines. Therefore, individuals and organizations need a systematic approach to prioritize effectively.

To prioritize tasks and goals effectively, the first step is identifying and evaluating the issue or job at hand. This involves gathering relevant data, analyzing it, and creating a list of proposed solutions. The initial evaluation helps determine the critical tasks and objectives and the extent of the work involved. The next step is to rank the potential solutions based on their urgency, importance, and feasibility. Individuals and organizations can prioritize their tasks and goals more efficiently and effectively by systematically evaluating and ranking the available options.

The **ABC approach** is an effective method for prioritizing tasks. It involves categorizing tasks as A, B, or C based on importance. **A tasks** are the most important and urgent, so they should be completed first. **B tasks** are significant but not urgent and can be addressed after A tasks. **C tasks** are neither necessary nor urgent and can be set aside. By prioritizing A tasks first, individuals and organizations can ensure that their most critical priorities are addressed.

An alternative approach to prioritization is the **Eisenhower matrix**, which sorts tasks into four categories based on their urgency and importance.

The **first category is urgent and essential tasks** that demand immediate attention. These tasks must be addressed first. Meanwhile, the **second category is necessary but not urgent tasks**, which can be scheduled and planned for later. Conversely, the **third category is urgent but unimportant tasks**, which can be delegated or delayed. Then the **fourth and final category is tasks that are not urgent or unimportant**, which can be dropped or postponed indefinitely. By categorizing tasks according to the Eisenhower matrix, individuals and organizations can optimize their time and resources for maximum efficiency and productivity.

A healthy balance between short-term and long-term objectives is necessary for effective prioritization. While focusing on urgent and critical tasks is essential, individuals and organizations must not neglect long-term goals. Failing long-term goals can result in missed opportunities and decreased productivity in the future. Therefore, individuals and organizations must allocate sufficient time and resources to achieve long-term goals while addressing immediate priorities.

To prioritize tasks effectively, communication and collaboration are essential. In organizations, it is critical to ensure that team members are clear about the priorities and that everyone works together. This helps to avoid duplication of efforts and ensures that resources are used effectively. Collaborating effectively allows team members to share the workload and achieve priorities quickly and efficiently.

Streamlining Processes and Eliminating Inefficiencies

Efficient processes and eliminating inefficiencies are critical for saving time, cutting costs, and improving output quality for individuals and organizations. With the constant pressure of achieving more with less, streamlining processes is a valuable tool. By eliminating inefficiencies and bottlenecks, individuals and organizations can achieve their objectives faster, save costs, and improve the quality of their output.

Process mapping is a powerful tool for streamlining processes. It involves mapping out the current process, identifying bottlenecks and inefficiencies, and creating a new, more efficient process. Likewise, it can help individuals and organizations identify areas where time and resources are wasted and develop new, streamlined processes.

First, process mapping identifies a process's inputs, actions, and outputs to understand its flow. The next step is to locate any bottlenecks and inefficiencies. This involves examining the process flow to identify delays, repetitions, or unnecessary stages. Individuals and organizations can create new, more streamlined, effective procedures by identifying these areas.

A manufacturing company can use process mapping to streamline its production process. First, the company can identify bottlenecks in the current process, such as delays in material delivery, inefficient machine setups, or unnecessary steps in the production line. By mapping out the process and identifying these inefficiencies, the company can develop a new process that reduces production time and costs while improving output quality.

Automation is also an effective method for streamlining processes. It entails using technology to automate repetitive or manual tasks. By automating these tasks, individuals and organizations can save time and reduce errors. This allows them to concentrate on higher-value activities, making their work more efficient.

Data entry, customer support, and inventory management are among the operations that can benefit from automation. For instance, a company can use automation to handle data entry tasks. Instead of manually inputting data into a system, the software can extract data from invoices, receipts, or forms. This approach saves time and reduces errors since manual data entry is prone to mistakes.

Moreover, automation can be applied in customer service as well. Chatbots, for example, can be used by businesses to respond to customer inquiries. Frequently asked questions can be programmed into chatbots, allowing customer service representatives to focus on more complex queries. Likewise, it improves the quality of customer service by handling inquiries promptly.

Streamlining processes and removing inefficiencies necessitates a mindset of constant improvement. Individuals and organizations must be willing to assess and improve their processes regularly. This entails gathering data, interpreting it, and changing the processes. Hence, staying competitive and achieving goals more effectively requires continuous process improvements.

Utilizing Available Resources Effectively and Efficiently

Resource allocation is a powerful technique for utilizing resources effectively. It involves distributing available resources, such as time, money, and employees, to accomplish the most critical activities or goals. **Prioritizing tasks and goals** is essential for optimal resource allocation. For instance, individuals and organizations must prioritize key issues based on their significance and viability, then allocate resources accordingly.

Suppose a company has multiple projects to complete. In such cases, they can prioritize them based on urgency and importance using a project management tool. By directing resources toward the most critical priorities, individuals and organizations can maximize their available resources and accomplish their desired goals more efficiently.

Another way to maximize resource utilization is through outsourcing. This involves hiring outside resources to handle specific tasks or projects. **Outsourcing** non-core functions allows individuals and organizations to save time and money while focusing on their core strengths. For example, a small business without a full-time IT staff may outsource IT services to another company. Besides that, it can help individuals and businesses reduce overhead costs, improve efficiency, and free up valuable resources.

To maximize their resources, implement technology and automation alongside resource allocation and outsourcing. By utilizing automation and technology, procedures can be streamlined, errors can be eliminated, and valuable resources can be freed up for other essential tasks. For instance, a company that relies on manual data entry could benefit from implementing an automated system. Automating repetitive or time-consuming tasks can save time and reduce errors, allowing individuals and organizations to focus on higher-value activities.

Maximizing resource utilization can also be achieved through cross-training, which involves preparing individuals to perform various organizational roles. This strategy ensures that key activities can still be executed, even if a team member is unavailable, by having a pool of employees equipped with the necessary skills and resources. In addition, cross-training promotes teamwork and collaboration as employees work together to acquire new skills and knowledge.

Optimal resource use requires ongoing review and monitoring. Individuals and organizations must continuously monitor their resource utilization and adjust their strategies as necessary. For instance, if a business is not meeting its desired outcomes, it may need to re-prioritize its tasks or reallocate resources to achieve its goals. Continuous monitoring and evaluation can help individuals and organizations identify inefficiencies and optimize resource utilization. By doing so, they can achieve their desired outcomes efficiently.

Creative Problem-Solving and Innovation

Creative problem-solving and innovation are crucial for managing time and resource limitations. They involve finding new and innovative solutions to problems and generating improved products, services, or processes. Other than that, it helps prioritize activities, simplify procedures, and effectively use resources.

The 4 Pillars of Problem-Solving

Conversely, brainstorming is an effective method for creative problem-solving. This technique involves generating many ideas quickly, without any bias or criticism. Through brainstorming, individuals and organizations can identify creative solutions to problems they may not have considered otherwise.

Another approach to creative problem-solving is design thinking, which prioritizes the needs and perspectives of users. By understanding the requirements and viewpoints of users, individuals, and organizations can develop more innovative and practical solutions to problems. This approach can lead to more user-friendly solutions and a higher chance of success.

Creating a culture of experimentation and learning is another effective way to promote innovation. When individuals and organizations encourage experimentation and learning, they can develop innovative solutions to problems and enhance their current products, services, and procedures. By embracing new approaches and promoting creativity, individuals and organizations can enhance their ability to innovate and find unique solutions.

Let us take an example of how these tactics can be implemented. Suppose a marketing team is given the responsibility of creating a new marketing campaign to promote a new product. They face a tight deadline and limited resources. To create a successful campaign, they must prioritize their activities, streamline their processes, and efficiently use their resources.

For instance, the marketing team employs the Eisenhower matrix and the ABC method to identify the essential tasks and prioritize them. To streamline their processes, the marketing team also uses process mapping. They identify bottlenecks and inefficiencies in their current marketing process and create a new, more streamlined method. Then, they also use resource allocation to assign resources to the most important tasks. Aside from that, they delegate non-core tasks such as graphic design and copywriting to save time and money.

By applying these strategies in practice, individuals and organizations can develop new and innovative solutions to problems, improve quality, reduce costs, and save time.

Conclusion

In conclusion, problem-solving is an essential skill that can be applied across various fields, including business, education, science, technology, medicine, and law.

In the first pillar, the focal point is understanding the problem and clearly defining the problem statement and objectives. This can be achieved through problem framing, data collection, and analysis techniques, and identifying causal and contributing factors. Gathering information is another critical aspect discussed, and it involves conducting research through surveys, interviews, observations, experiments, and simulations.

The second pillar of problem-solving is strategizing, which involves using flowcharts, diagrams, and SWOT analysis to determine the purpose and scope of the problem, identify the process, and evaluate the strengths, weaknesses, opportunities, and threats. Six Sigma methodology is also helpful in strategizing, as it involves the DMAIC process of defining, measuring, analyzing, improving, and controlling.

Moreover, the third pillar explains deciding, identifying options, and evaluating and prioritizing solutions. Brainstorming sessions, probability analysis, and idea generation workshops help identify options, while decision matrices, decision trees, and multi-criteria decision analysis help evaluate and prioritize solutions. Assessing risk and uncertainty and refining and selecting the best solution is also necessary for making decisions.

The final pillar of problem-solving is overcoming, which involves addressing issues such as lack of clarity, biases, assumptions, and time and resource constraints. To overcome these challenges, it is essential to break down the problem, question assumptions and biases, prioritize tasks and goals, streamline processes, and utilize available resources effectively and efficiently.

Overall, effective problem-solving requires a systematic approach that involves understanding the problem, strategizing, deciding, and overcoming it. It also requires critical thinking, creativity, and innovation. Being an effective problem-solver is a skill that can be developed and refined with practice. With the right mindset, tools, and techniques, you can become a skilled problem solver and positively impact your field.

Glossary

ABC Method: A method used to prioritize and analyze important issues by ranking them from most to least important, with A given top priority.

Accountability: The ability to be responsible for one's actions, which can also refer to holding someone accountable for their actions to prevent them from repeating them.

Action Plan: A plan of action consisting of specific steps to achieve a goal or objective.

Adoption of Appropriate Responses: Suitable or appropriate responses for a given situation or problem, which may be positive or negative, depending on what is needed to resolve the issue.

Cognitive Biases: The tendency to think or act in a certain way due to personal biases, such as trusting people who look or sound like us.

Communication: The act of imparting knowledge to others, consisting of written, verbal, and nonverbal elements.

Contributing Factors: Factors that contribute to the occurrence of something, such as education, intelligence, personality traits, motivation, and self-esteem, in the case of creativity.

Creative Problem-Solving: A problem-solving method that generates multiple solutions before choosing the best option in decision-making situations with insufficient information.

Critical Path Diagram: A diagram showing the time required to complete a project and the necessary tasks to meet that deadline.

Critical Thinking: The capacity to evaluate data and draw judgments based on reason, logic, and evidence, applicable to decision-making across all aspects of life.

Data Analysis: The process of collecting, organizing, analyzing, interpreting, and communicating data to gain insight into a situation or problem for various purposes, such as identifying trends, evaluating effectiveness, predicting future behavior, and identifying areas for improvement.

Decision Matrices: A tool for structuring decisions that breaks down each option into categories and rates each category on a scale. This helps identify the most desirable options while still allowing for confident decision-making.

Decision-making: The process of using information to make choices.

Defects per million opportunities (DPMO): The ratio of a product's total number of faults to the number of possibilities for product problems. This is used to assess whether a product meets its quality objectives.

Design for Six Sigma (DFSS): A methodology for designing products and services that meet customer needs while minimizing defects.

Design thinking: A problem-solving approach that considers users' needs and context when designing products or services.

Diagrams: Visual representations of data that communicate information clearly and effectively.

The 4 Pillars of Problem-Solving

Divide and conquer: A problem-solving strategy that breaks down complex problems into smaller, manageable parts.

DMAIC: A problem-solving process that involves defining the problem, measuring its extent, analyzing its causes, implementing an improvement plan, and ensuring the improvement stays in place over time.

Effective problem-solving: A process of looking at multiple perspectives on a problem before coming up with a solution.

Efficiency: The amount of output that can be produced for each unit of input used in manufacturing.

Eisenhower matrix: A chart for prioritizing tasks based on importance vs. urgency and whether they are actionable.

Evaluation criteria: Standards of quality or performance used to determine whether something is ready for production or use by customers/clients.

Evaluation: The process of deciding whether a problem has been solved or whether to keep looking for solutions.

Experiment: A process of trying different approaches or materials to solve a problem.

Feedback: Information provided about the effectiveness of a solution.

Flow charts: Graphical representations that illustrate the steps of a process, helping to identify potential issues and facilitate their resolution.

Four pillars of effective problem-solving: A problem-solving framework that includes four steps: defining the problem, brainstorming possible solutions, selecting and implementing a solution, and evaluating the solution's effectiveness.

Gantt Chart: A chart that displays tasks by date and time over an extended period, typically weeks, enabling visualization of what needs to be done and when, to ensure timely completion.

Groupthink: A phenomenon that occurs when a group agrees to come together to solve a problem, making it challenging to think outside the box and often resulting in a suboptimal solution.

Holistic approach: An approach to problem-solving that considers all aspects of a problem simultaneously rather than only focusing on one aspect.

Improve phase: A stage of the problem-solving process where ways to enhance overall efficiency and effectiveness are identified to avoid repeating unnecessary steps or spending too much time on any one task.

Innovation: Originality or the ability to create something new and different from what existed before, often linked to creativity and unique thinking.

Interdependencies: The relationship between two or more things that are mutually connected or dependent on each other.

Iterative feedback and testing: A problem-solving approach where feedback is gathered from clients or stakeholders after each project iteration, and changes are made based on that feedback.

Limitations and considerations: Potential challenges or drawbacks associated with a particular approach or method, which may result in delays in product delivery.

Merge sort algorithm: An algorithm for sorting data that uses divide-and-conquer logic to reduce a large list into smaller lists, which are then merged to create even smaller lists until all data is sorted.

The 4 Pillars of Problem-Solving

Milestones: Interim goals that mark progress towards a long-term objective, typically used in Integrated software development projects to track progress.

Multi-criteria decision analysis (MCDA): A decision-making method that evaluates options against different criteria within a given situation, often used in business and government applications.

Outsourcing: The practice of hiring a third party to complete a task or project that would typically be handled by an internal team.

Pairwise comparison: A decision-making method where two possibilities are compared simultaneously to identify the optimal choice.

Problem statement: A statement that describes a problem, issue, or challenge that needs to be resolved, including information about its components (who, what, where, when, why, and how).

Problem-solving abilities: Skills and knowledge that help someone effectively solve problems for themselves or others.

Problem-solving process: The steps taken to successfully complete a task or project.

Problem-solving: A process that involves using logical reasoning and creative thinking to find solutions to problems.

Process Flowcharts: Illustrations that show the steps involved in a process and can be used to depict information or material flow, or workflow.

Process Mapping: An activity that uses process flowcharts to understand how processes work and identify areas for improvement.

Resource allocation: The practice of assigning resources such as time or money to a specific project, task, or person.

Resource constraints: Limits on the availability of resources that impact project performance.

Responsibility Assignment Matrix (RAM): A tool used by businesses to designate who is responsible for specific duties within a project plan, often used with Gantt charts.

Risk assessment: A process of analyzing potential risks before beginning a project to determine their likelihood and potential impact on project success.

Root cause analysis: A process of identifying the underlying causes of an issue and developing a plan to address them.

Root cause: A description of what happened, along with recommendations for how to prevent it from happening again in the future.

Simulation: A model used to imitate a real-world situation for testing different scenarios and determining optimal outcomes.

Six Sigma: A statistical-based quality management system that aims to improve processes significantly.

SMART: An abbreviation for Specific, Measurable, Achievable, Relevant, and Time-bound, used for setting milestones.

Stakeholders: Individuals or groups with a personal stake in a project's success and may be affected by it at different stages.

Streamlining: A process for reducing the number of steps in a process by eliminating unnecessary stages or combining them into a single phase.

Sub-problems: Lesser issues that must be resolved to address the main issue, which should be identified and addressed efficiently.

Swimlane diagrams: A type of flowchart where each step is assigned to one person or group of people (called "swimmers"). The swimmer's responsibilities are displayed alongside their swimlane on the diagram. Swimlane diagrams help visualize how work will be divided up among different groups of people and show which tasks are dependent upon each other.

SWOT analysis: An analysis conducted before starting any project that identifies weaknesses, strengths, opportunities, and threats related to the project. The purpose of SWOT analysis is to identify these factors beforehand so that teams can strategize ways to capitalize on their strengths while minimizing the impact of their weaknesses or taking advantage of opportunities.

Systematic approach: A method of planning or organizing the steps needed to complete a task. The systematic approach is often used by businesses when they are looking to come up with new ideas or improve existing products or services.

Targeted solution: A solution that is focused on solving a specific problem or issue.

Utility analysis: An evaluation tool that helps companies determine how much value their products and services have. Utility analysis can be used as part of the development process to ensure a new product is viable before it hits the market.

Viability: The likelihood of something being successful in its current state, given its current resources and environment.

Weighting schemes: Methods for determining how important different factors are when making decisions about something. Weighting schemes can be used when evaluating products and services to determine the features most benefit customers.

References

American Psychological Association. (2020). Publication manual of the American Psychological Association (7th ed.).

Arora, M. (2019). *Indispensable Lean and Six Sigma Tools and Techniques.* Medium. https://arorameghna.medium.com/indispensable-lean-and-six-sigma-tools-and-techniques-8bb337ca9f4

Bowerman, B. L., O'Connell, R. T., & Orris, J. B. (2018). Probability and statistics for engineering and the sciences. Cengage Learning.

Bucaro, M. (2020). Visual Design Solutions: Principles and Creative Inspiration for Learning Professionals. John Wiley & Sons.

Collegenp. (2023). *Three Major Theories of Motivation: Understanding Maslow, Herzberg, and Self-Determination.* Www.collegenp.com. https://www.collegenp.com/motivation/three-major-theories-of-motivation

DFSS | Design for Six Sigma | Quality-One. (2015). Quality-One.com. https://quality-one.com/dfss/

DuBrin, A. J. (2021). Principles of leadership. Cengage Learning.

Ellis, D. B., & Abbott, J. (2021). Becoming a master student. Cengage Learning.

Erdogan, S. A. (2020). Multiple Criteria Decision Analysis. In N. M. Seel (Ed.), Encyclopedia of the Sciences of Learning (pp. 2231-2233). Springer.

Godsey, J. (2010). *A Business Plan for an Organic Restaurant.* https://digitalcommons.calpoly.edu/cgi/viewcontent.cgi?article=1035&context=agbsp

Greco, S., Matarazzo, B., & Slowinski, R. (2016). Multiple criteria decision analysis: State of the art surveys (2nd ed.). Springer.

Hill, T., & Westbrook, R. (1997). SWOT analysis: It's time for a product recall. Long Range Planning, 30(1), 46-52.

Humphrey, A. (1960). SWOT analysis for management planning. Journal of Long Range Planning, 2(2), 46-52.

Jex, S. M., & Britt, T. W. (2014). Organizational psychology: A scientist-practitioner approach. John Wiley & Sons.

Jones, M. (2019). Creative brainstorming techniques. In J. Smith (Ed.), Business creativity and innovation for managers (pp. 45-67). Wiley-Blackwell.

Jones, R. (2020). problem-solving: Techniques, Strategies & Methods. New York: McGraw-Hill Education.

Jones, T. (2019). Design thinking in practice. New York, NY: Routledge.

Kothari, C. R. (2004). Research methodology: Methods and techniques. New Age International.

Lacerda, T. (2020). Resource Allocation. In S. G. Rogelberg (Ed.), The SAGE Encyclopedia of Industrial and Organizational Psychology (2nd ed., pp. 1171-1173). SAGE Publications, Inc.

Larson, E. W., & Gray, C. F. (2021). Project management: The managerial process. McGraw-Hill Education.

Morris, C. G., & Maisto, A. A. (2017). Understanding Psychology (12th ed.). Pearson.

Mosley, M. (2020). Mind mapping: Unlock your creativity and boost your productivity. DK Publishing.

Prabhakaran, S. (2023). *Fishbone Diagram*. Prabhakaran.io. https://www.prabhakaran.io/post/fishbone-diagram

Pyzdek, T., & Keller, P. A. (2014). The six sigma handbook: A complete guide for green belts, black belts, and managers at all levels (3rd ed.). McGraw-Hill Education.

Robbins, S. P., & Judge, T. A. (2021). Organizational behavior (18th ed.). Pearson.

Scherer, L. L., & Jackson, T. L. (2019). Business decision making. John Wiley & Sons.

Simon, B., Garlick, R., & Beare, P. (2021). Problem-solving and decision-making: A guide for managers. Kogan Page Publishers.

Six Sigma Certifications - Starting Only $49 - Affordable Certifications, Free Books! 50% Off Until Early Next Week! (n.d.). International Six Sigma Institute. https://www.sixsigma-institute.org/How_Does_Six_Sigma_DMAIC_Process_Work.php

Smith, A. B., & Johnson, C. D. (2020). Data collection methods. In Research Methods for Business and Social Science Students (pp. 123-142). Routledge.

Smith, A., & Johnson, B. (2021). Data Analysis Techniques: A Beginner's Guide. Wiley.

Smith, J. (2018). Decision Trees. In J. Doe (Ed.), Handbook of Decision Making (pp. 123-145). Publisher.

Smith, J. (2020). Open and honest dialogue: Addressing biases and presumptions. In K. Brown (Ed.), Strategies for Effective Decision-Making (pp. 45-57). Wiley.

Smith, J. (2022). Data analysis for business. Publisher.

Smith, J. D., & Merritt, S. (2021). Decision-Making Strategies for Project Management. New York, NY: McGraw Hill.

Smith, J., & Jones, M. (2020). Business problem-solving: A practical guide. McGraw-Hill.

Sternberg, R. J. (2018). Cognitive psychology (7th ed.). Cengage Learning.

SWOT Analysis. (n.d.). Mr Deniz Ates | Boxing Training. https://www.mrdenizates.com/blog/swot-analysis

Tidd, J., & Bessant, J. (2018). Managing innovation: Integrating technological, market and organizational change (6th ed.). John Wiley & Sons.

Walter, D., & Smith, M. (2019). Eisenhower's Urgent/Important Principle: Using Time Effectively, Not Just Efficiently. In Time Management for System Administrators (pp. 33-42). O'Reilly Media.

Wlodkowski, R. J., & Ginsberg, M. B. (2017). Enhancing adult motivation to learn: A comprehensive guide for teaching all adults. Jossey-Bass.

Made in the USA
Las Vegas, NV
02 November 2024